D1541529

The HOCKEY Journal

created by
Jody M. Anderson

Big Pond Books
an imprint of Lake 7 Creative, LLC
Minneapolis, Minnesota

SPECIAL THANKS:

A big "Thank You" to Stephanie Opdahl, April Rudek, and Lynn Yerigan. Your ideas and input were greatly appreciated.

Book and cover design by Ryan Jacobson

All images from Shutterstock.com

10 9 8 7 6 5 4 3 2 1

Copyright 2014 by Jody M. Anderson
Published by Big Pond Books
an imprint of Lake 7 Creative, LLC
Minneapolis, MN 55412
www.bigpondbooks.com

All rights reserved
Printed in the U.S.A.

ISBN: 978-1-940647-10-4

Introduction

I always thought it would be great to track my kids' hockey progress. It would be a helpful tool to improve their games. It would also be a lasting memory—sort of like a yearbook. We could look back at the teams and at how much fun it was to be at certain arenas and, of course, the tournaments!

I didn't have it for my own children, but I'm passing the idea along to you. Bring this journal to hockey games (and even to practices). Log your child's progress, and then, at the end of the year, you'll see how much they improved.

The Hockey Journal may even encourage them to do their hockey homework. If they know that you're keeping track of their progress, they'll be that much more motivated to put in extra time on their own.

Let your hockey star use the journal, too. There's room at the end to get team autographs. Oh, what fun it'll be to look back on this book, years down the road. I'm so jealous . . . but at least I can use *The Hockey Journal* with my grandchildren!

—Jody M. Anderson

How to Use

Following are most of the journal fields for you to fill in. Many are self-explanatory, but I've provided a brief description of each so you can see what I had in mind. Of course, these are just suggestions. Use the journal however you see fit.

Team: There's room to note your team, especially if it might change from season to season.

Date: The month/day/year of the event.

Location: Note the arena and the city (state and country).

Opponent: What team are you playing? Or is it practice?

Individual: If you're tracking more than one person in the same journal, write down the player's name here.

Position: At what position did you first play? Did you change positions during the game? Log that, too.

Line: Were you on the first, second, or third line? If you moved up or down, be sure to note that.

Goals: How many did you score?

Assists: How many goals were scored after a pass from you?

Points: Add your total goals and assists together.

Power Play Goals: How many goals did you score while the other team had fewer players on the ice?

Power Play Assists: How many assists did you get while the other team had fewer players on the ice?

Shorthanded Goals: How many goals did you score while the other team had more players on the ice?

Shorthanded Assists: How many assists did you get while the other team had more players on the ice?

Faceoffs: How many faceoffs did you take part in (the start of a play, when a puck is dropped between two players)?

Faceoff Wins: How many times did you get the puck for your team during a faceoff?

Takeaways: How many times did you take the puck away from an opponent?

Giveaways: How many times did an opponent take the puck away from you?

Shots on Goal: How many shots did you take? (For it to count, the shot has to enter the crease area, which is usually outlined in front of the goal.)

Plus/Minus: Add a plus sign (+) when your team scores a goal while you're on the ice. Add a minus sign (-) if you're on the ice when the other team scores.

Penalties in Minutes: How many minutes did you serve in the penalty box?

Time on Ice: How much total time did you spend on the ice?

Goals Against: How many goals were scored against you while you were playing goalie?

Shots on Goal: How many shots did opponents take against you? (Include goals and all shots that enter the crease area.)

Saves: How many shots did you stop from scoring?

Save percentage: Divide number of saves by shots on goal. Multiply that number times 100. ($8 \div 10 \times 100 = 80\%$)

Total Minutes: How much time did you play goalie?

W-L-T: Did your team win, lose, or tie?

Notes: Write a short game summary and/or mention anything noteworthy that happened with your child.

TEAM:

Date: _____ Location: _____

Opponent (or Practice): _____

Score by Period: _____ _____ _____ _____ _____
                    1   2   3   OT   F

INDIVIDUAL:

Position: _____ Line: _____

Goals: _____ Assists: _____ Points: _____

Power Play Goals: _____ Power Play Assists: _____

Shorthanded Goals: _____ Shorthanded Assists: _____

Faceoffs: _____ Faceoff Wins: _____

Takeaways: _____ Giveaways: _____

Shots on Goal: _____ Plus/Minus: _____ / _____

Penalties in Minutes: _____ Time on Ice: _____

GOALTENDER:

Goals Against: _____ Shots on Goal: _____

Saves: _____ Save Percentage: _____

Total Minutes: _____ W-L-T: _____

NOTES: _____

_____

_____

_____

TEAM:

Date: _____   Location: _____

Opponent (or Practice): _____

Score by Period: _____ _____ _____ _____ _____
                    1   2   3   OT   F

INDIVIDUAL:

Position: _____   Line: _____

Goals: _____   Assists: _____   Points: _____

Power Play Goals: _____   Power Play Assists: _____

Shorthanded Goals: _____   Shorthanded Assists: _____

Faceoffs: _____   Faceoff Wins: _____

Takeaways: _____   Giveaways: _____

Shots on Goal: _____   Plus/Minus: _____ / _____

Penalties in Minutes: _____   Time on Ice: _____

GOALTENDER:

Goals Against: _____   Shots on Goal: _____

Saves: _____   Save Percentage: _____

Total Minutes: _____   W-L-T: _____

NOTES: _____

_____

_____

_____

TEAM:

Date: _____ Location: _____

Opponent (or Practice): _____

Score by Period: _____ _____ _____ _____ _____
                        1   2   3   OT   F

INDIVIDUAL:

Position: _____ Line: _____

Goals: _____ Assists: _____ Points: _____

Power Play Goals: _____ Power Play Assists: _____

Shorthanded Goals: _____ Shorthanded Assists: _____

Faceoffs: _____ Faceoff Wins: _____

Takeaways: _____ Giveaways: _____

Shots on Goal: _____ Plus/Minus: _____/_____

Penalties in Minutes: _____ Time on Ice: _____

GOALTENDER:

Goals Against: _____ Shots on Goal: _____

Saves: _____ Save Percentage: _____

Total Minutes: _____ W-L-T: _____

NOTES: _____

_____

_____

_____

Team:

Date: _____ Location: _____

Opponent (or Practice): _____

Score by Period: _____ _____ _____ _____ _____
                                  1   2   3   OT   F

Individual:

Position: _____ Line: _____

Goals: _____ Assists: _____ Points: _____

Power Play Goals: _____ Power Play Assists: _____

Shorthanded Goals: _____ Shorthanded Assists: _____

Faceoffs: _____ Faceoff Wins: _____

Takeaways: _____ Giveaways: _____

Shots on Goal: _____ Plus/Minus: _____ / _____

Penalties in Minutes: _____ Time on Ice: _____

Goaltender:

Goals Against: _____ Shots on Goal: _____

Saves: _____ Save Percentage: _____

Total Minutes: _____ W-L-T: _____

Notes: _____

_____

_____

_____

TEAM:

Date: _____ Location: _____

Opponent (or Practice): _____

Score by Period: _____ _____ _____ _____ _____
                    1   2   3   OT   F

INDIVIDUAL:

Position: _____ Line: _____

Goals: _____ Assists: _____ Points: _____

Power Play Goals: _____ Power Play Assists: _____

Shorthanded Goals: _____ Shorthanded Assists: _____

Faceoffs: _____ Faceoff Wins: _____

Takeaways: _____ Giveaways: _____

Shots on Goal: _____ Plus/Minus: _____ / _____

Penalties in Minutes: _____ Time on Ice: _____

GOALTENDER:

Goals Against: _____ Shots on Goal: _____

Saves: _____ Save Percentage: _____

Total Minutes: _____ W-L-T: _____

NOTES: _____

_____

_____

_____

TEAM:

Date: _____ Location: _____

Opponent (or Practice): _____

Score by Period: _____ _____ _____ _____ _____
                    1   2   3   OT   F

INDIVIDUAL:

Position: _____ Line: _____

Goals: _____ Assists: _____ Points: _____

Power Play Goals: _____ Power Play Assists: _____

Shorthanded Goals: _____ Shorthanded Assists: _____

Faceoffs: _____ Faceoff Wins: _____

Takeaways: _____ Giveaways: _____

Shots on Goal: _____ Plus/Minus: _____ / _____

Penalties in Minutes: _____ Time on Ice: _____

GOALTENDER:

Goals Against: _____ Shots on Goal: _____

Saves: _____ Save Percentage: _____

Total Minutes: _____ W-L-T: _____

NOTES: _____

_____

_____

_____

TEAM:

Date: _____ Location: _____

Opponent (or Practice): _____

Score by Period: _____ _____ _____ _____ _____
                   1   2   3   OT   F

INDIVIDUAL:

Position: _____ Line: _____

Goals: _____ Assists: _____ Points: _____

Power Play Goals: _____ Power Play Assists: _____

Shorthanded Goals: _____ Shorthanded Assists: _____

Faceoffs: _____ Faceoff Wins: _____

Takeaways: _____ Giveaways: _____

Shots on Goal: _____ Plus/Minus: _____ / _____

Penalties in Minutes: _____ Time on Ice: _____

GOALTENDER:

Goals Against: _____ Shots on Goal: _____

Saves: _____ Save Percentage: _____

Total Minutes: _____ W-L-T: _____

NOTES: _____

_____

_____

_____

TEAM:

Date: _____ Location: _____

Opponent (or Practice): _____

Score by Period: _____ _____ _____ _____ _____
                   1   2   3   OT   F

INDIVIDUAL:

Position: _____ Line: _____

Goals: _____ Assists: _____ Points: _____

Power Play Goals: _____ Power Play Assists: _____

Shorthanded Goals: _____ Shorthanded Assists: _____

Faceoffs: _____ Faceoff Wins: _____

Takeaways: _____ Giveaways: _____

Shots on Goal: _____ Plus/Minus: _____ / _____

Penalties in Minutes: _____ Time on Ice: _____

GOALTENDER:

Goals Against: _____ Shots on Goal: _____

Saves: _____ Save Percentage: _____

Total Minutes: _____ W-L-T: _____

NOTES: _____

_____

_____

_____

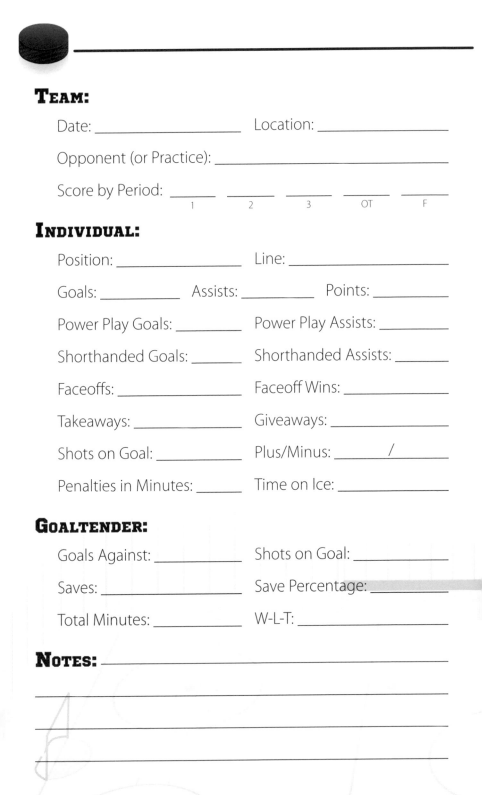

Team:

Date: _____ Location: _____

Opponent (or Practice): _____

Score by Period: _____ _____ _____ _____ _____
                    1   2   3   OT   F

Individual:

Position: _____ Line: _____

Goals: _____ Assists: _____ Points: _____

Power Play Goals: _____ Power Play Assists: _____

Shorthanded Goals: _____ Shorthanded Assists: _____

Faceoffs: _____ Faceoff Wins: _____

Takeaways: _____ Giveaways: _____

Shots on Goal: _____ Plus/Minus: _____ / _____

Penalties in Minutes: _____ Time on Ice: _____

Goaltender:

Goals Against: _____ Shots on Goal: _____

Saves: _____ Save Percentage: _____

Total Minutes: _____ W-L-T: _____

Notes: _____

_____

_____

_____

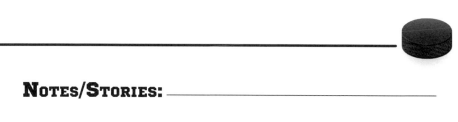

NOTES/STORIES: _____

TEAM:

Date: _____ Location: _____

Opponent (or Practice): _____

Score by Period: _____ _____ _____ _____ _____
                                 1   2   3   OT   F

INDIVIDUAL:

Position: _____ Line: _____

Goals: _____ Assists: _____ Points: _____

Power Play Goals: _____ Power Play Assists: _____

Shorthanded Goals: _____ Shorthanded Assists: _____

Faceoffs: _____ Faceoff Wins: _____

Takeaways: _____ Giveaways: _____

Shots on Goal: _____ Plus/Minus: _____/_____

Penalties in Minutes: _____ Time on Ice: _____

GOALTENDER:

Goals Against: _____ Shots on Goal: _____

Saves: _____ Save Percentage: _____

Total Minutes: _____ W-L-T: _____

NOTES: _____

_____

_____

_____

TEAM:

Date: _____ Location: _____

Opponent (or Practice): _____

Score by Period: _____ _____ _____ _____ _____
                     1   2   3   OT   F

INDIVIDUAL:

Position: _____ Line: _____

Goals: _____ Assists: _____ Points: _____

Power Play Goals: _____ Power Play Assists: _____

Shorthanded Goals: _____ Shorthanded Assists: _____

Faceoffs: _____ Faceoff Wins: _____

Takeaways: _____ Giveaways: _____

Shots on Goal: _____ Plus/Minus: _____ / _____

Penalties in Minutes: _____ Time on Ice: _____

GOALTENDER:

Goals Against: _____ Shots on Goal: _____

Saves: _____ Save Percentage: _____

Total Minutes: _____ W-L-T: _____

NOTES: _____

_____

_____

_____

TEAM:

Date: _____ Location: _____

Opponent (or Practice): _____

Score by Period: _____ _____ _____ _____ _____
₁   ₂   ₃   OT   F

INDIVIDUAL:

Position: _____ Line: _____

Goals: _____ Assists: _____ Points: _____

Power Play Goals: _____ Power Play Assists: _____

Shorthanded Goals: _____ Shorthanded Assists: _____

Faceoffs: _____ Faceoff Wins: _____

Takeaways: _____ Giveaways: _____

Shots on Goal: _____ Plus/Minus: _____/_____

Penalties in Minutes: _____ Time on Ice: _____

GOALTENDER:

Goals Against: _____ Shots on Goal: _____

Saves: _____ Save Percentage: _____

Total Minutes: _____ W-L-T: _____

NOTES: _____

_____

_____

_____

Team:

Date: _____ Location: _____

Opponent (or Practice): _____

Score by Period: _____ _____ _____ _____ _____
            1   2   3   OT   F

Individual:

Position: _____ Line: _____

Goals: _____ Assists: _____ Points: _____

Power Play Goals: _____ Power Play Assists: _____

Shorthanded Goals: _____ Shorthanded Assists: _____

Faceoffs: _____ Faceoff Wins: _____

Takeaways: _____ Giveaways: _____

Shots on Goal: _____ Plus/Minus: _____ / _____

Penalties in Minutes: _____ Time on Ice: _____

Goaltender:

Goals Against: _____ Shots on Goal: _____

Saves: _____ Save Percentage: _____

Total Minutes: _____ W-L-T: _____

Notes: _____

_____

_____

_____

TEAM:

Date: _____ Location: _____

Opponent (or Practice): _____

Score by Period: _____ _____ _____ _____ _____
　　　　　　　　　　1　　　　2　　　　3　　　　OT　　　　F

INDIVIDUAL:

Position: _____ Line: _____

Goals: _____ Assists: _____ Points: _____

Power Play Goals: _____ Power Play Assists: _____

Shorthanded Goals: _____ Shorthanded Assists: _____

Faceoffs: _____ Faceoff Wins: _____

Takeaways: _____ Giveaways: _____

Shots on Goal: _____ Plus/Minus: _____ / _____

Penalties in Minutes: _____ Time on Ice: _____

GOALTENDER:

Goals Against: _____ Shots on Goal: _____

Saves: _____ Save Percentage: _____

Total Minutes: _____ W-L-T: _____

NOTES: _____

_____

_____

_____

TEAM:

Date: _____ Location: _____

Opponent (or Practice): _____

Score by Period: _____ _____ _____ _____ _____
                    1   2   3   OT   F

INDIVIDUAL:

Position: _____ Line: _____

Goals: _____ Assists: _____ Points: _____

Power Play Goals: _____ Power Play Assists: _____

Shorthanded Goals: _____ Shorthanded Assists: _____

Faceoffs: _____ Faceoff Wins: _____

Takeaways: _____ Giveaways: _____

Shots on Goal: _____ Plus/Minus: _____ / _____

Penalties in Minutes: _____ Time on Ice: _____

GOALTENDER:

Goals Against: _____ Shots on Goal: _____

Saves: _____ Save Percentage: _____

Total Minutes: _____ W-L-T: _____

NOTES: _____

_____

_____

_____

TEAM:

Date: _____ Location: _____

Opponent (or Practice): _____

Score by Period: _____ _____ _____ _____ _____
                    1   2   3   OT   F

INDIVIDUAL:

Position: _____ Line: _____

Goals: _____ Assists: _____ Points: _____

Power Play Goals: _____ Power Play Assists: _____

Shorthanded Goals: _____ Shorthanded Assists: _____

Faceoffs: _____ Faceoff Wins: _____

Takeaways: _____ Giveaways: _____

Shots on Goal: _____ Plus/Minus: _____ / _____

Penalties in Minutes: _____ Time on Ice: _____

GOALTENDER:

Goals Against: _____ Shots on Goal: _____

Saves: _____ Save Percentage: _____

Total Minutes: _____ W-L-T: _____

NOTES: _____

_____

_____

_____

Team:

Date: _____ Location: _____

Opponent (or Practice): _____

Score by Period: _____ _____ _____ _____ _____
                    1   2   3   OT   F

Individual:

Position: _____ Line: _____

Goals: _____ Assists: _____ Points: _____

Power Play Goals: _____ Power Play Assists: _____

Shorthanded Goals: _____ Shorthanded Assists: _____

Faceoffs: _____ Faceoff Wins: _____

Takeaways: _____ Giveaways: _____

Shots on Goal: _____ Plus/Minus: _____ / _____

Penalties in Minutes: _____ Time on Ice: _____

Goaltender:

Goals Against: _____ Shots on Goal: _____

Saves: _____ Save Percentage: _____

Total Minutes: _____ W-L-T: _____

Notes: _____

_____

_____

_____

TEAM:

Date: _____ Location: _____

Opponent (or Practice): _____

Score by Period: _____ _____ _____ _____ _____
                        1   2   3   OT   F

INDIVIDUAL:

Position: _____ Line: _____

Goals: _____ Assists: _____ Points: _____

Power Play Goals: _____ Power Play Assists: _____

Shorthanded Goals: _____ Shorthanded Assists: _____

Faceoffs: _____ Faceoff Wins: _____

Takeaways: _____ Giveaways: _____

Shots on Goal: _____ Plus/Minus: _____ / _____

Penalties in Minutes: _____ Time on Ice: _____

GOALTENDER:

Goals Against: _____ Shots on Goal: _____

Saves: _____ Save Percentage: _____

Total Minutes: _____ W-L-T: _____

NOTES: _____

_____

_____

_____

TEAM:

Date: _____ Location: _____

Opponent (or Practice): _____

Score by Period: _____ _____ _____ _____ _____
                    1   2   3   OT   F

INDIVIDUAL:

Position: _____ Line: _____

Goals: _____ Assists: _____ Points: _____

Power Play Goals: _____ Power Play Assists: _____

Shorthanded Goals: _____ Shorthanded Assists: _____

Faceoffs: _____ Faceoff Wins: _____

Takeaways: _____ Giveaways: _____

Shots on Goal: _____ Plus/Minus: _____/_____

Penalties in Minutes: _____ Time on Ice: _____

GOALTENDER:

Goals Against: _____ Shots on Goal: _____

Saves: _____ Save Percentage: _____

Total Minutes: _____ W-L-T: _____

NOTES: _____

_____

_____

_____

TEAM:

Date: _____ Location: _____

Opponent (or Practice): _____

Score by Period: _____ _____ _____ _____ _____
                                  1   2   3   OT   F

INDIVIDUAL:

Position: _____ Line: _____

Goals: _____ Assists: _____ Points: _____

Power Play Goals: _____ Power Play Assists: _____

Shorthanded Goals: _____ Shorthanded Assists: _____

Faceoffs: _____ Faceoff Wins: _____

Takeaways: _____ Giveaways: _____

Shots on Goal: _____ Plus/Minus: _____/_____

Penalties in Minutes: _____ Time on Ice: _____

GOALTENDER:

Goals Against: _____ Shots on Goal: _____

Saves: _____ Save Percentage: _____

Total Minutes: _____ W-L-T: _____

NOTES: _____

_____

_____

_____

NOTES/STORIES:

TEAM:

Date: _____ Location: _____

Opponent (or Practice): _____

Score by Period: _____ _____ _____ _____ _____
                                 1   2   3   OT   F

INDIVIDUAL:

Position: _____ Line: _____

Goals: _____ Assists: _____ Points: _____

Power Play Goals: _____ Power Play Assists: _____

Shorthanded Goals: _____ Shorthanded Assists: _____

Faceoffs: _____ Faceoff Wins: _____

Takeaways: _____ Giveaways: _____

Shots on Goal: _____ Plus/Minus: _____/_____

Penalties in Minutes: _____ Time on Ice: _____

GOALTENDER:

Goals Against: _____ Shots on Goal: _____

Saves: _____ Save Percentage: _____

Total Minutes: _____ W-L-T: _____

NOTES: _____

_____

_____

_____

Team:

Date: _____ Location: _____

Opponent (or Practice): _____

Score by Period: _____ _____ _____ _____ _____
1   2   3   OT   F

Individual:

Position: _____ Line: _____

Goals: _____ Assists: _____ Points: _____

Power Play Goals: _____ Power Play Assists: _____

Shorthanded Goals: _____ Shorthanded Assists: _____

Faceoffs: _____ Faceoff Wins: _____

Takeaways: _____ Giveaways: _____

Shots on Goal: _____ Plus/Minus: _____ / _____

Penalties in Minutes: _____ Time on Ice: _____

Goaltender:

Goals Against: _____ Shots on Goal: _____

Saves: _____ Save Percentage: _____

Total Minutes: _____ W-L-T: _____

Notes: _____

_____

_____

_____

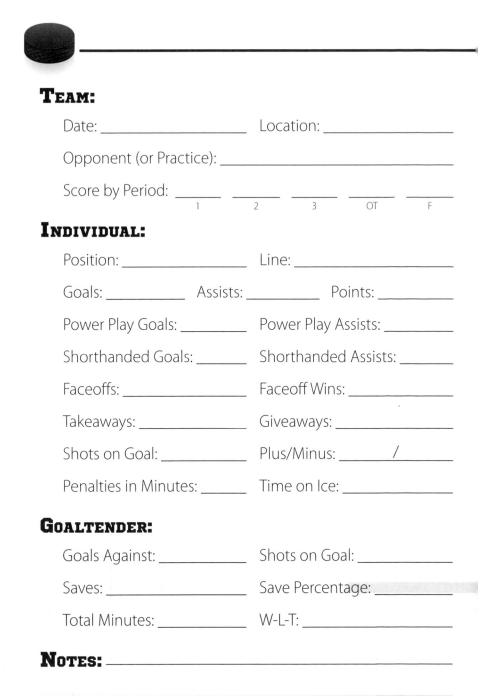

TEAM:

Date: _____ Location: _____

Opponent (or Practice): _____

Score by Period: _____ _____ _____ _____ _____
                    1   2   3   OT   F

INDIVIDUAL:

Position: _____ Line: _____

Goals: _____ Assists: _____ Points: _____

Power Play Goals: _____ Power Play Assists: _____

Shorthanded Goals: _____ Shorthanded Assists: _____

Faceoffs: _____ Faceoff Wins: _____

Takeaways: _____ Giveaways: _____

Shots on Goal: _____ Plus/Minus: _____/_____

Penalties in Minutes: _____ Time on Ice: _____

GOALTENDER:

Goals Against: _____ Shots on Goal: _____

Saves: _____ Save Percentage: _____

Total Minutes: _____ W-L-T: _____

NOTES: _____

_____

_____

_____

TEAM:

Date: _____ Location: _____

Opponent (or Practice): _____

Score by Period: _____ _____ _____ _____ _____
                    1   2   3   OT   F

INDIVIDUAL:

Position: _____ Line: _____

Goals: _____ Assists: _____ Points: _____

Power Play Goals: _____ Power Play Assists: _____

Shorthanded Goals: _____ Shorthanded Assists: _____

Faceoffs: _____ Faceoff Wins: _____

Takeaways: _____ Giveaways: _____

Shots on Goal: _____ Plus/Minus: _____ / _____

Penalties in Minutes: _____ Time on Ice: _____

GOALTENDER:

Goals Against: _____ Shots on Goal: _____

Saves: _____ Save Percentage: _____

Total Minutes: _____ W-L-T: _____

NOTES: _____

_____

_____

_____

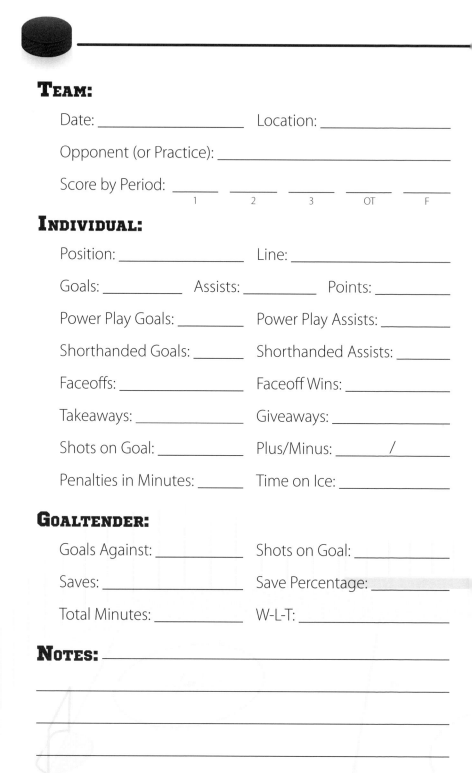

TEAM:

Date: _____ Location: _____

Opponent (or Practice): _____

Score by Period: _____ _____ _____ _____ _____
                        1   2   3   OT   F

INDIVIDUAL:

Position: _____ Line: _____

Goals: _____ Assists: _____ Points: _____

Power Play Goals: _____ Power Play Assists: _____

Shorthanded Goals: _____ Shorthanded Assists: _____

Faceoffs: _____ Faceoff Wins: _____

Takeaways: _____ Giveaways: _____

Shots on Goal: _____ Plus/Minus: _____ / _____

Penalties in Minutes: _____ Time on Ice: _____

GOALTENDER:

Goals Against: _____ Shots on Goal: _____

Saves: _____ Save Percentage: _____

Total Minutes: _____ W-L-T: _____

NOTES: _____

_____

_____

_____

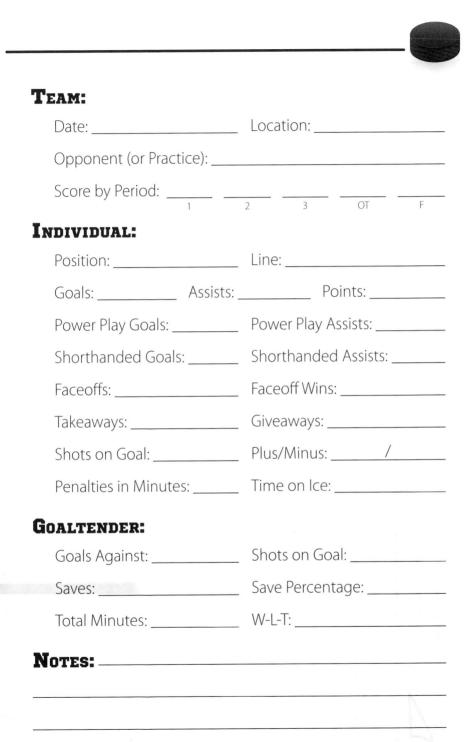

Team:

Date: _____ Location: _____

Opponent (or Practice): _____

Score by Period: _____ _____ _____ _____ _____
                    1   2   3   OT   F

Individual:

Position: _____ Line: _____

Goals: _____ Assists: _____ Points: _____

Power Play Goals: _____ Power Play Assists: _____

Shorthanded Goals: _____ Shorthanded Assists: _____

Faceoffs: _____ Faceoff Wins: _____

Takeaways: _____ Giveaways: _____

Shots on Goal: _____ Plus/Minus: _____ / _____

Penalties in Minutes: _____ Time on Ice: _____

Goaltender:

Goals Against: _____ Shots on Goal: _____

Saves: _____ Save Percentage: _____

Total Minutes: _____ W-L-T: _____

Notes: _____

_____

_____

_____

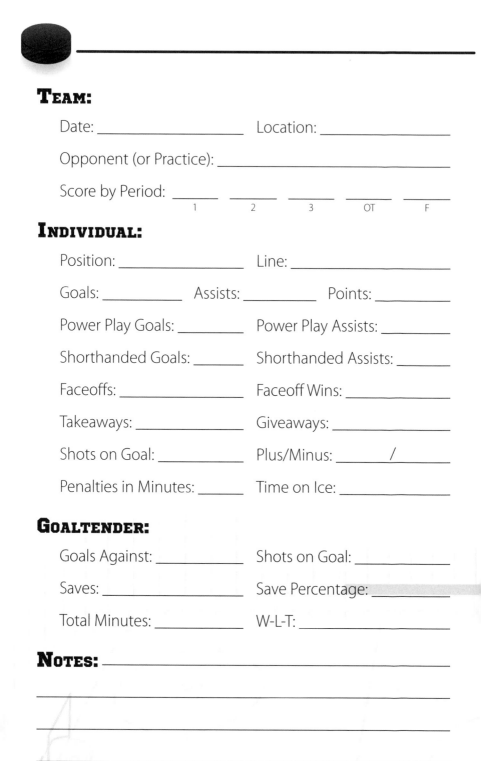

TEAM:

Date: _____ Location: _____

Opponent (or Practice): _____

Score by Period: _____ _____ _____ _____ _____
                    1   2   3   OT   F

INDIVIDUAL:

Position: _____ Line: _____

Goals: _____ Assists: _____ Points: _____

Power Play Goals: _____ Power Play Assists: _____

Shorthanded Goals: _____ Shorthanded Assists: _____

Faceoffs: _____ Faceoff Wins: _____

Takeaways: _____ Giveaways: _____

Shots on Goal: _____ Plus/Minus: _____ / _____

Penalties in Minutes: _____ Time on Ice: _____

GOALTENDER:

Goals Against: _____ Shots on Goal: _____

Saves: _____ Save Percentage: _____

Total Minutes: _____ W-L-T: _____

NOTES: _____

_____

_____

_____

Team:

Date: _____ Location: _____

Opponent (or Practice): _____

Score by Period: _____ _____ _____ _____ _____
                    1   2   3   OT   F

Individual:

Position: _____ Line: _____

Goals: _____ Assists: _____ Points: _____

Power Play Goals: _____ Power Play Assists: _____

Shorthanded Goals: _____ Shorthanded Assists: _____

Faceoffs: _____ Faceoff Wins: _____

Takeaways: _____ Giveaways: _____

Shots on Goal: _____ Plus/Minus: _____ / _____

Penalties in Minutes: _____ Time on Ice: _____

Goaltender:

Goals Against: _____ Shots on Goal: _____

Saves: _____ Save Percentage: _____

Total Minutes: _____ W-L-T: _____

Notes: _____

_____

_____

_____

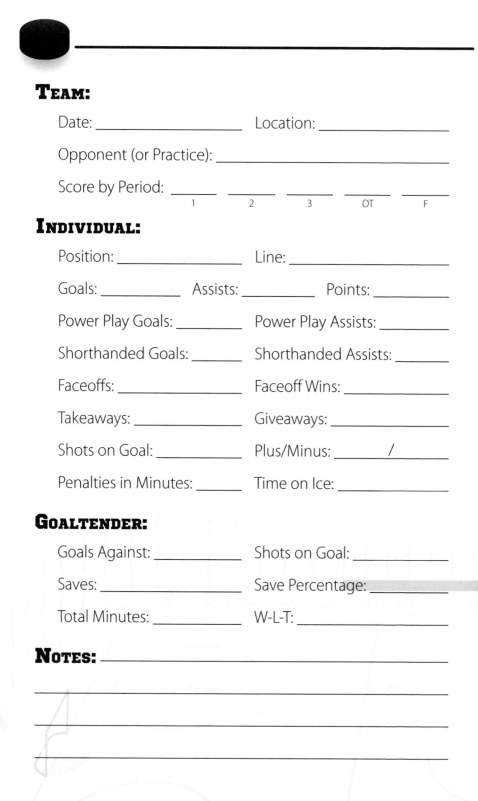

TEAM:

Date: _____ Location: _____

Opponent (or Practice): _____

Score by Period: _____ _____ _____ _____ _____
　　　　　　　　　　　　1　　　　2　　　　3　　　OT　　　F

INDIVIDUAL:

Position: _____ Line: _____

Goals: _____ Assists: _____ Points: _____

Power Play Goals: _____ Power Play Assists: _____

Shorthanded Goals: _____ Shorthanded Assists: _____

Faceoffs: _____ Faceoff Wins: _____

Takeaways: _____ Giveaways: _____

Shots on Goal: _____ Plus/Minus: _____ / _____

Penalties in Minutes: _____ Time on Ice: _____

GOALTENDER:

Goals Against: _____ Shots on Goal: _____

Saves: _____ Save Percentage: _____

Total Minutes: _____ W-L-T: _____

NOTES: _____

_____

_____

_____

TEAM:

Date: _____ Location: _____

Opponent (or Practice): _____

Score by Period: _____ _____ _____ _____ _____
                         1   2   3   OT   F

INDIVIDUAL:

Position: _____ Line: _____

Goals: _____ Assists: _____ Points: _____

Power Play Goals: _____ Power Play Assists: _____

Shorthanded Goals: _____ Shorthanded Assists: _____

Faceoffs: _____ Faceoff Wins: _____

Takeaways: _____ Giveaways: _____

Shots on Goal: _____ Plus/Minus: _____ / _____

Penalties in Minutes: _____ Time on Ice: _____

GOALTENDER:

Goals Against: _____ Shots on Goal: _____

Saves: _____ Save Percentage: _____

Total Minutes: _____ W-L-T: _____

NOTES: _____

_____

_____

_____

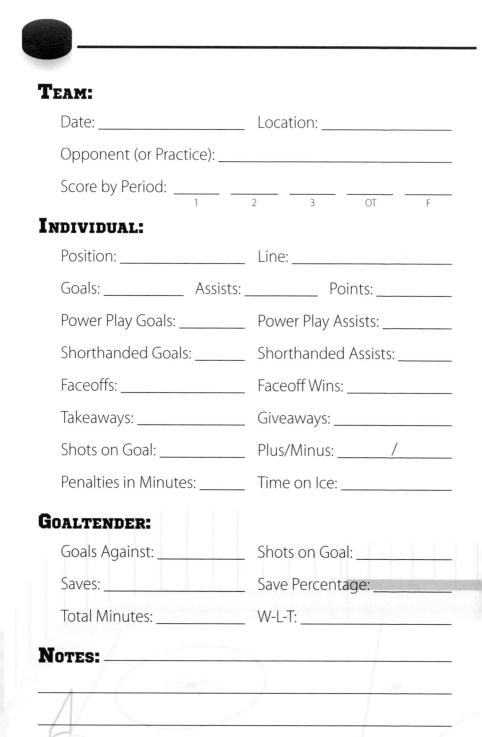

TEAM:

Date: _____ Location: _____

Opponent (or Practice): _____

Score by Period: _____ _____ _____ _____ _____
$\qquad$ 1 $\qquad$ 2 $\qquad$ 3 $\qquad$ OT $\qquad$ F

INDIVIDUAL:

Position: _____ Line: _____

Goals: _____ Assists: _____ Points: _____

Power Play Goals: _____ Power Play Assists: _____

Shorthanded Goals: _____ Shorthanded Assists: _____

Faceoffs: _____ Faceoff Wins: _____

Takeaways: _____ Giveaways: _____

Shots on Goal: _____ Plus/Minus: _____ / _____

Penalties in Minutes: _____ Time on Ice: _____

GOALTENDER:

Goals Against: _____ Shots on Goal: _____

Saves: _____ Save Percentage: _____

Total Minutes: _____ W-L-T: _____

NOTES: _____

_____

_____

_____

NOTES/STORIES:

TEAM:

Date: _____ Location: _____

Opponent (or Practice): _____

Score by Period: _____ _____ _____ _____ _____
                   1   2   3   OT   F

INDIVIDUAL:

Position: _____ Line: _____

Goals: _____ Assists: _____ Points: _____

Power Play Goals: _____ Power Play Assists: _____

Shorthanded Goals: _____ Shorthanded Assists: _____

Faceoffs: _____ Faceoff Wins: _____

Takeaways: _____ Giveaways: _____

Shots on Goal: _____ Plus/Minus: _____ / _____

Penalties in Minutes: _____ Time on Ice: _____

GOALTENDER:

Goals Against: _____ Shots on Goal: _____

Saves: _____ Save Percentage: _____

Total Minutes: _____ W-L-T: _____

NOTES: _____

_____

_____

_____

TEAM:

Date: _____ Location: _____

Opponent (or Practice): _____

Score by Period: _____ _____ _____ _____ _____
                    1   2   3   OT   F

INDIVIDUAL:

Position: _____ Line: _____

Goals: _____ Assists: _____ Points: _____

Power Play Goals: _____ Power Play Assists: _____

Shorthanded Goals: _____ Shorthanded Assists: _____

Faceoffs: _____ Faceoff Wins: _____

Takeaways: _____ Giveaways: _____

Shots on Goal: _____ Plus/Minus: _____ / _____

Penalties in Minutes: _____ Time on Ice: _____

GOALTENDER:

Goals Against: _____ Shots on Goal: _____

Saves: _____ Save Percentage: _____

Total Minutes: _____ W-L-T: _____

NOTES: _____

_____

_____

_____

TEAM:

Date: _____ Location: _____

Opponent (or Practice): _____

Score by Period: _____ _____ _____ _____ _____
                     1   2   3   OT   F

INDIVIDUAL:

Position: _____ Line: _____

Goals: _____ Assists: _____ Points: _____

Power Play Goals: _____ Power Play Assists: _____

Shorthanded Goals: _____ Shorthanded Assists: _____

Faceoffs: _____ Faceoff Wins: _____

Takeaways: _____ Giveaways: _____

Shots on Goal: _____ Plus/Minus: _____ / _____

Penalties in Minutes: _____ Time on Ice: _____

GOALTENDER:

Goals Against: _____ Shots on Goal: _____

Saves: _____ Save Percentage: _____

Total Minutes: _____ W-L-T: _____

NOTES: _____

_____

_____

_____

Team:

Date: _____ Location: _____

Opponent (or Practice): _____

Score by Period: _____ _____ _____ _____ _____
                     1   2   3   OT   F

Individual:

Position: _____ Line: _____

Goals: _____ Assists: _____ Points: _____

Power Play Goals: _____ Power Play Assists: _____

Shorthanded Goals: _____ Shorthanded Assists: _____

Faceoffs: _____ Faceoff Wins: _____

Takeaways: _____ Giveaways: _____

Shots on Goal: _____ Plus/Minus: _____ / _____

Penalties in Minutes: _____ Time on Ice: _____

Goaltender:

Goals Against: _____ Shots on Goal: _____

Saves: _____ Save Percentage: _____

Total Minutes: _____ W-L-T: _____

Notes: _____

_____

_____

_____

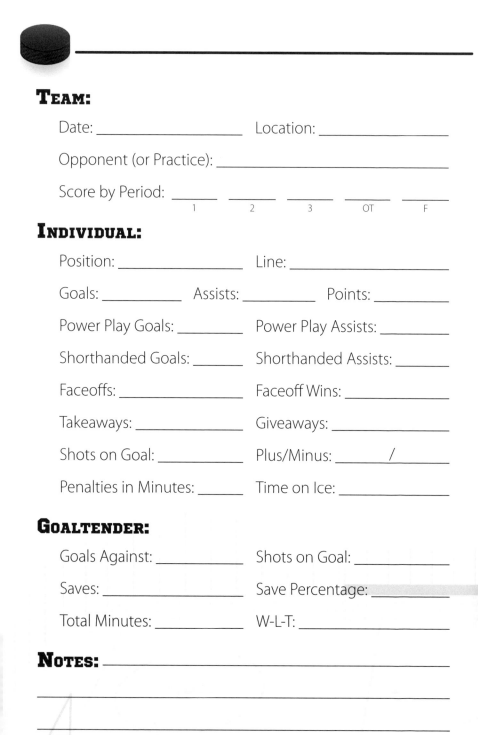

Team:

Date: _____   Location: _____

Opponent (or Practice): _____

Score by Period: _____ _____ _____ _____ _____
                    1   2   3   OT   F

Individual:

Position: _____   Line: _____

Goals: _____ Assists: _____ Points: _____

Power Play Goals: _____   Power Play Assists: _____

Shorthanded Goals: _____   Shorthanded Assists: _____

Faceoffs: _____   Faceoff Wins: _____

Takeaways: _____   Giveaways: _____

Shots on Goal: _____   Plus/Minus: _____ / _____

Penalties in Minutes: _____   Time on Ice: _____

Goaltender:

Goals Against: _____   Shots on Goal: _____

Saves: _____   Save Percentage: _____

Total Minutes: _____   W-L-T: _____

Notes: _____

_____

_____

_____

TEAM:

Date: _____ Location: _____

Opponent (or Practice): _____

Score by Period: _____ _____ _____ _____ _____
                    1   2   3   OT   F

INDIVIDUAL:

Position: _____ Line: _____

Goals: _____ Assists: _____ Points: _____

Power Play Goals: _____ Power Play Assists: _____

Shorthanded Goals: _____ Shorthanded Assists: _____

Faceoffs: _____ Faceoff Wins: _____

Takeaways: _____ Giveaways: _____

Shots on Goal: _____ Plus/Minus: _____/_____

Penalties in Minutes: _____ Time on Ice: _____

GOALTENDER:

Goals Against: _____ Shots on Goal: _____

Saves: _____ Save Percentage: _____

Total Minutes: _____ W-L-T: _____

NOTES: _____

_____

_____

_____

TEAM:

Date: _____ Location: _____

Opponent (or Practice): _____

Score by Period: _____ _____ _____ _____ _____
                          1   2   3   OT   F

INDIVIDUAL:

Position: _____ Line: _____

Goals: _____ Assists: _____ Points: _____

Power Play Goals: _____ Power Play Assists: _____

Shorthanded Goals: _____ Shorthanded Assists: _____

Faceoffs: _____ Faceoff Wins: _____

Takeaways: _____ Giveaways: _____

Shots on Goal: _____ Plus/Minus: _____ / _____

Penalties in Minutes: _____ Time on Ice: _____

GOALTENDER:

Goals Against: _____ Shots on Goal: _____

Saves: _____ Save Percentage: _____

Total Minutes: _____ W-L-T: _____

NOTES: _____

_____

_____

_____

Team:

Date: _____ Location: _____

Opponent (or Practice): _____

Score by Period: _____ _____ _____ _____ _____
                    1   2   3   OT   F

Individual:

Position: _____ Line: _____

Goals: _____ Assists: _____ Points: _____

Power Play Goals: _____ Power Play Assists: _____

Shorthanded Goals: _____ Shorthanded Assists: _____

Faceoffs: _____ Faceoff Wins: _____

Takeaways: _____ Giveaways: _____

Shots on Goal: _____ Plus/Minus: _____ / _____

Penalties in Minutes: _____ Time on Ice: _____

Goaltender:

Goals Against: _____ Shots on Goal: _____

Saves: _____ Save Percentage: _____

Total Minutes: _____ W-L-T: _____

Notes: _____

_____

_____

_____

TEAM:

Date: _____ Location: _____

Opponent (or Practice): _____

Score by Period: _____ _____ _____ _____ _____
　　　　　　　　　　　1　　　　2　　　　3　　　OT　　　F

INDIVIDUAL:

Position: _____ Line: _____

Goals: _____ Assists: _____ Points: _____

Power Play Goals: _____ Power Play Assists: _____

Shorthanded Goals: _____ Shorthanded Assists: _____

Faceoffs: _____ Faceoff Wins: _____

Takeaways: _____ Giveaways: _____

Shots on Goal: _____ Plus/Minus: _____/_____

Penalties in Minutes: _____ Time on Ice: _____

GOALTENDER:

Goals Against: _____ Shots on Goal: _____

Saves: _____ Save Percentage: _____

Total Minutes: _____ W-L-T: _____

NOTES: _____

_____

_____

_____

Team:

Date: _____ Location: _____

Opponent (or Practice): _____

Score by Period: _____ _____ _____ _____ _____
                   1   2   3   OT   F

Individual:

Position: _____ Line: _____

Goals: _____ Assists: _____ Points: _____

Power Play Goals: _____ Power Play Assists: _____

Shorthanded Goals: _____ Shorthanded Assists: _____

Faceoffs: _____ Faceoff Wins: _____

Takeaways: _____ Giveaways: _____

Shots on Goal: _____ Plus/Minus: _____/_____

Penalties in Minutes: _____ Time on Ice: _____

Goaltender:

Goals Against: _____ Shots on Goal: _____

Saves: _____ Save Percentage: _____

Total Minutes: _____ W-L-T: _____

Notes: _____

_____

_____

_____

TEAM:

Date: _____ Location: _____

Opponent (or Practice): _____

Score by Period: _____ _____ _____ _____ _____
                    1   2   3   OT   F

INDIVIDUAL:

Position: _____ Line: _____

Goals: _____ Assists: _____ Points: _____

Power Play Goals: _____ Power Play Assists: _____

Shorthanded Goals: _____ Shorthanded Assists: _____

Faceoffs: _____ Faceoff Wins: _____

Takeaways: _____ Giveaways: _____

Shots on Goal: _____ Plus/Minus: _____ / _____

Penalties in Minutes: _____ Time on Ice: _____

GOALTENDER:

Goals Against: _____ Shots on Goal: _____

Saves: _____ Save Percentage: _____

Total Minutes: _____ W-L-T: _____

NOTES: _____

_____

_____

_____

NOTES/STORIES:

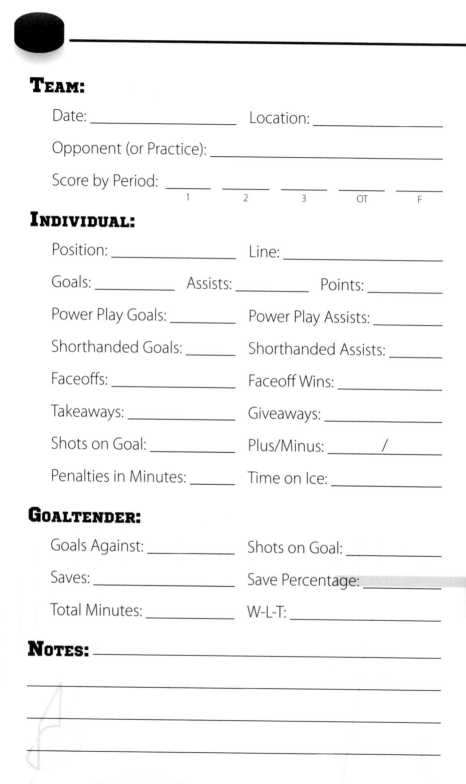

TEAM:

Date: _____ Location: _____

Opponent (or Practice): _____

Score by Period: _____ _____ _____ _____ _____
　　　　　　　　　　　1　　　2　　　3　　　OT　　　F

INDIVIDUAL:

Position: _____ Line: _____

Goals: _____ Assists: _____ Points: _____

Power Play Goals: _____ Power Play Assists: _____

Shorthanded Goals: _____ Shorthanded Assists: _____

Faceoffs: _____ Faceoff Wins: _____

Takeaways: _____ Giveaways: _____

Shots on Goal: _____ Plus/Minus: _____ / _____

Penalties in Minutes: _____ Time on Ice: _____

GOALTENDER:

Goals Against: _____ Shots on Goal: _____

Saves: _____ Save Percentage: _____

Total Minutes: _____ W-L-T: _____

NOTES: _____

_____

_____

_____

TEAM:

Date: _____ Location: _____

Opponent (or Practice): _____

Score by Period: _____ _____ _____ _____ _____
　　　　　　　　　　　1　　　　2　　　　3　　　OT　　　F

INDIVIDUAL:

Position: _____ Line: _____

Goals: _____ Assists: _____ Points: _____

Power Play Goals: _____ Power Play Assists: _____

Shorthanded Goals: _____ Shorthanded Assists: _____

Faceoffs: _____ Faceoff Wins: _____

Takeaways: _____ Giveaways: _____

Shots on Goal: _____ Plus/Minus: _____/_____

Penalties in Minutes: _____ Time on Ice: _____

GOALTENDER:

Goals Against: _____ Shots on Goal: _____

Saves: _____ Save Percentage: _____

Total Minutes: _____ W-L-T: _____

NOTES: _____

_____

_____

_____

TEAM:

Date: _____ Location: _____

Opponent (or Practice): _____

Score by Period: _____ _____ _____ _____ _____
                    1   2   3   OT   F

INDIVIDUAL:

Position: _____ Line: _____

Goals: _____ Assists: _____ Points: _____

Power Play Goals: _____ Power Play Assists: _____

Shorthanded Goals: _____ Shorthanded Assists: _____

Faceoffs: _____ Faceoff Wins: _____

Takeaways: _____ Giveaways: _____

Shots on Goal: _____ Plus/Minus: _____/_____

Penalties in Minutes: _____ Time on Ice: _____

GOALTENDER:

Goals Against: _____ Shots on Goal: _____

Saves: _____ Save Percentage: _____

Total Minutes: _____ W-L-T: _____

NOTES: _____

_____

_____

_____

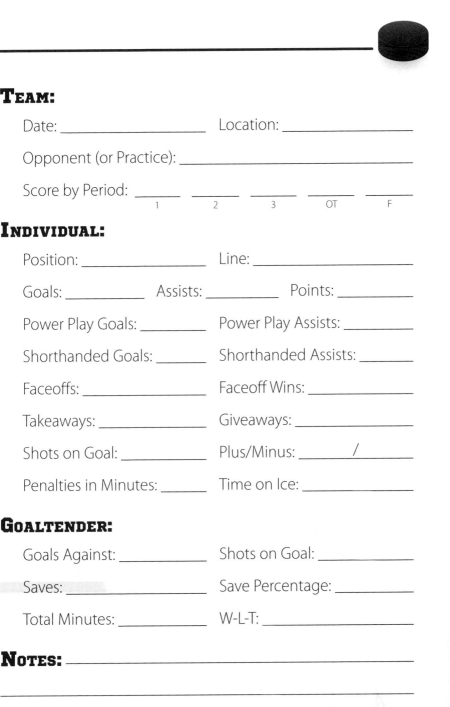

TEAM:

Date: _____ Location: _____

Opponent (or Practice): _____

Score by Period: _____ _____ _____ _____ _____
                    1   2   3   OT   F

INDIVIDUAL:

Position: _____ Line: _____

Goals: _____ Assists: _____ Points: _____

Power Play Goals: _____ Power Play Assists: _____

Shorthanded Goals: _____ Shorthanded Assists: _____

Faceoffs: _____ Faceoff Wins: _____

Takeaways: _____ Giveaways: _____

Shots on Goal: _____ Plus/Minus: _____ / _____

Penalties in Minutes: _____ Time on Ice: _____

GOALTENDER:

Goals Against: _____ Shots on Goal: _____

Saves: _____ Save Percentage: _____

Total Minutes: _____ W-L-T: _____

NOTES: _____

_____

_____

_____

Team:

Date: _____ Location: _____

Opponent (or Practice): _____

Score by Period: _____ _____ _____ _____ _____
                       1   2   3   OT   F

Individual:

Position: _____ Line: _____

Goals: _____ Assists: _____ Points: _____

Power Play Goals: _____ Power Play Assists: _____

Shorthanded Goals: _____ Shorthanded Assists: _____

Faceoffs: _____ Faceoff Wins: _____

Takeaways: _____ Giveaways: _____

Shots on Goal: _____ Plus/Minus: _____/_____

Penalties in Minutes: _____ Time on Ice: _____

Goaltender:

Goals Against: _____ Shots on Goal: _____

Saves: _____ Save Percentage: _____

Total Minutes: _____ W-L-T: _____

Notes: _____

_____

_____

_____

Team:

Date: _____ Location: _____

Opponent (or Practice): _____

Score by Period: _____ _____ _____ _____ _____
                    1   2   3   OT   F

Individual:

Position: _____ Line: _____

Goals: _____ Assists: _____ Points: _____

Power Play Goals: _____ Power Play Assists: _____

Shorthanded Goals: _____ Shorthanded Assists: _____

Faceoffs: _____ Faceoff Wins: _____

Takeaways: _____ Giveaways: _____

Shots on Goal: _____ Plus/Minus: _____ / _____

Penalties in Minutes: _____ Time on Ice: _____

Goaltender:

Goals Against: _____ Shots on Goal: _____

Saves: _____ Save Percentage: _____

Total Minutes: _____ W-L-T: _____

Notes: _____

_____

_____

_____

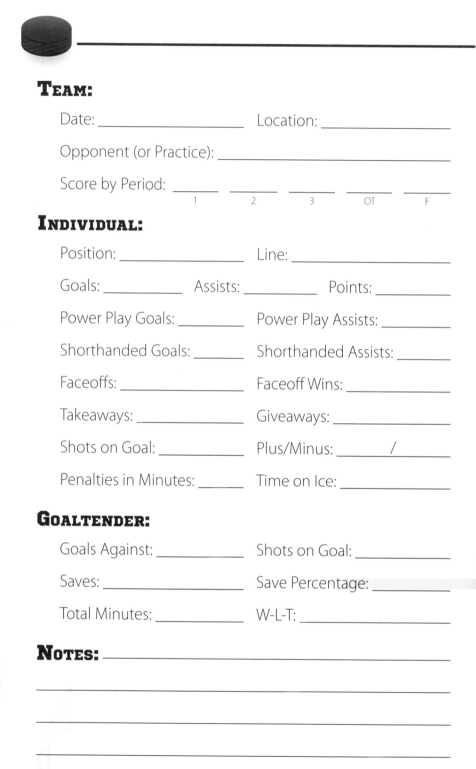

TEAM:

Date: _____ Location: _____

Opponent (or Practice): _____

Score by Period: _____ _____ _____ _____ _____
                             1   2   3   OT   F

INDIVIDUAL:

Position: _____ Line: _____

Goals: _____ Assists: _____ Points: _____

Power Play Goals: _____ Power Play Assists: _____

Shorthanded Goals: _____ Shorthanded Assists: _____

Faceoffs: _____ Faceoff Wins: _____

Takeaways: _____ Giveaways: _____

Shots on Goal: _____ Plus/Minus: _____ / _____

Penalties in Minutes: _____ Time on Ice: _____

GOALTENDER:

Goals Against: _____ Shots on Goal: _____

Saves: _____ Save Percentage: _____

Total Minutes: _____ W-L-T: _____

NOTES: _____

_____

_____

_____

Team:

Date: _____ Location: _____

Opponent (or Practice): _____

Score by Period: _____ _____ _____ _____ _____
                   1   2   3   OT   F

Individual:

Position: _____ Line: _____

Goals: _____ Assists: _____ Points: _____

Power Play Goals: _____ Power Play Assists: _____

Shorthanded Goals: _____ Shorthanded Assists: _____

Faceoffs: _____ Faceoff Wins: _____

Takeaways: _____ Giveaways: _____

Shots on Goal: _____ Plus/Minus: _____/_____

Penalties in Minutes: _____ Time on Ice: _____

Goaltender:

Goals Against: _____ Shots on Goal: _____

Saves: _____ Save Percentage: _____

Total Minutes: _____ W-L-T: _____

Notes: _____

_____

_____

_____

TEAM:

Date: _____ Location: _____

Opponent (or Practice): _____

Score by Period: _____ _____ _____ _____ _____
                    1   2   3   OT   F

INDIVIDUAL:

Position: _____ Line: _____

Goals: _____ Assists: _____ Points: _____

Power Play Goals: _____ Power Play Assists: _____

Shorthanded Goals: _____ Shorthanded Assists: _____

Faceoffs: _____ Faceoff Wins: _____

Takeaways: _____ Giveaways: _____

Shots on Goal: _____ Plus/Minus: _____ / _____

Penalties in Minutes: _____ Time on Ice: _____

GOALTENDER:

Goals Against: _____ Shots on Goal: _____

Saves: _____ Save Percentage: _____

Total Minutes: _____ W-L-T: _____

NOTES: _____

_____

_____

_____

Team:

Date: _____ Location: _____

Opponent (or Practice): _____

Score by Period: _____ _____ _____ _____ _____
                    1   2   3   OT   F

Individual:

Position: _____ Line: _____

Goals: _____ Assists: _____ Points: _____

Power Play Goals: _____ Power Play Assists: _____

Shorthanded Goals: _____ Shorthanded Assists: _____

Faceoffs: _____ Faceoff Wins: _____

Takeaways: _____ Giveaways: _____

Shots on Goal: _____ Plus/Minus: _____ / _____

Penalties in Minutes: _____ Time on Ice: _____

Goaltender:

Goals Against: _____ Shots on Goal: _____

Saves: _____ Save Percentage: _____

Total Minutes: _____ W-L-T: _____

Notes: _____

_____

_____

_____

TEAM:

Date: _____ Location: _____

Opponent (or Practice): _____

Score by Period: _____ _____ _____ _____ _____
                     1   2   3   OT   F

INDIVIDUAL:

Position: _____ Line: _____

Goals: _____ Assists: _____ Points: _____

Power Play Goals: _____ Power Play Assists: _____

Shorthanded Goals: _____ Shorthanded Assists: _____

Faceoffs: _____ Faceoff Wins: _____

Takeaways: _____ Giveaways: _____

Shots on Goal: _____ Plus/Minus: _____ / _____

Penalties in Minutes: _____ Time on Ice: _____

GOALTENDER:

Goals Against: _____ Shots on Goal: _____

Saves: _____ Save Percentage: _____

Total Minutes: _____ W-L-T: _____

NOTES: _____

_____

_____

_____

Notes/Stories:

TEAM:

Date: _____ Location: _____

Opponent (or Practice): _____

Score by Period: _____ _____ _____ _____ _____
1   2   3   OT   F

INDIVIDUAL:

Position: _____ Line: _____

Goals: _____ Assists: _____ Points: _____

Power Play Goals: _____ Power Play Assists: _____

Shorthanded Goals: _____ Shorthanded Assists: _____

Faceoffs: _____ Faceoff Wins: _____

Takeaways: _____ Giveaways: _____

Shots on Goal: _____ Plus/Minus: _____ / _____

Penalties in Minutes: _____ Time on Ice: _____

GOALTENDER:

Goals Against: _____ Shots on Goal: _____

Saves: _____ Save Percentage: _____

Total Minutes: _____ W-L-T: _____

NOTES: _____

_____

_____

_____

TEAM:

Date: _____ Location: _____

Opponent (or Practice): _____

Score by Period: _____ _____ _____ _____ _____
                    1   2   3   OT   F

INDIVIDUAL:

Position: _____ Line: _____

Goals: _____ Assists: _____ Points: _____

Power Play Goals: _____ Power Play Assists: _____

Shorthanded Goals: _____ Shorthanded Assists: _____

Faceoffs: _____ Faceoff Wins: _____

Takeaways: _____ Giveaways: _____

Shots on Goal: _____ Plus/Minus: _____ / _____

Penalties in Minutes: _____ Time on Ice: _____

GOALTENDER:

Goals Against: _____ Shots on Goal: _____

Saves: _____ Save Percentage: _____

Total Minutes: _____ W-L-T: _____

NOTES: _____

_____

_____

_____

TEAM:

Date: _____ Location: _____

Opponent (or Practice): _____

Score by Period: _____ _____ _____ _____ _____
                         1   2   3   OT   F

INDIVIDUAL:

Position: _____ Line: _____

Goals: _____ Assists: _____ Points: _____

Power Play Goals: _____ Power Play Assists: _____

Shorthanded Goals: _____ Shorthanded Assists: _____

Faceoffs: _____ Faceoff Wins: _____

Takeaways: _____ Giveaways: _____

Shots on Goal: _____ Plus/Minus: _____/_____

Penalties in Minutes: _____ Time on Ice: _____

GOALTENDER:

Goals Against: _____ Shots on Goal: _____

Saves: _____ Save Percentage: _____

Total Minutes: _____ W-L-T: _____

NOTES: _____

_____

_____

_____

TEAM:

Date: _____ Location: _____

Opponent (or Practice): _____

Score by Period: _____ _____ _____ _____ _____
                           1   2   3   OT   F

INDIVIDUAL:

Position: _____ Line: _____

Goals: _____ Assists: _____ Points: _____

Power Play Goals: _____ Power Play Assists: _____

Shorthanded Goals: _____ Shorthanded Assists: _____

Faceoffs: _____ Faceoff Wins: _____

Takeaways: _____ Giveaways: _____

Shots on Goal: _____ Plus/Minus: _____/_____

Penalties in Minutes: _____ Time on Ice: _____

GOALTENDER:

Goals Against: _____ Shots on Goal: _____

Saves: _____ Save Percentage: _____

Total Minutes: _____ W-L-T: _____

NOTES: _____

_____

_____

_____

TEAM:

Date: _____ Location: _____

Opponent (or Practice): _____

Score by Period: _____ _____ _____ _____ _____
                                 1   2   3   OT   F

INDIVIDUAL:

Position: _____ Line: _____

Goals: _____ Assists: _____ Points: _____

Power Play Goals: _____ Power Play Assists: _____

Shorthanded Goals: _____ Shorthanded Assists: _____

Faceoffs: _____ Faceoff Wins: _____

Takeaways: _____ Giveaways: _____

Shots on Goal: _____ Plus/Minus: _____ / _____

Penalties in Minutes: _____ Time on Ice: _____

GOALTENDER:

Goals Against: _____ Shots on Goal: _____

Saves: _____ Save Percentage: _____

Total Minutes: _____ W-L-T: _____

NOTES: _____

_____

_____

_____

TEAM:

Date: _____ Location: _____

Opponent (or Practice): _____

Score by Period: _____ _____ _____ _____ _____
                              1   2   3   OT   F

INDIVIDUAL:

Position: _____ Line: _____

Goals: _____ Assists: _____ Points: _____

Power Play Goals: _____ Power Play Assists: _____

Shorthanded Goals: _____ Shorthanded Assists: _____

Faceoffs: _____ Faceoff Wins: _____

Takeaways: _____ Giveaways: _____

Shots on Goal: _____ Plus/Minus: _____ / _____

Penalties in Minutes: _____ Time on Ice: _____

GOALTENDER:

Goals Against: _____ Shots on Goal: _____

Saves: _____ Save Percentage: _____

Total Minutes: _____ W-L-T: _____

NOTES: _____

_____

_____

_____

TEAM:

Date: _____ Location: _____

Opponent (or Practice): _____

Score by Period: _____ _____ _____ _____ _____
  1   2   3   OT   F

INDIVIDUAL:

Position: _____ Line: _____

Goals: _____ Assists: _____ Points: _____

Power Play Goals: _____ Power Play Assists: _____

Shorthanded Goals: _____ Shorthanded Assists: _____

Faceoffs: _____ Faceoff Wins: _____

Takeaways: _____ Giveaways: _____

Shots on Goal: _____ Plus/Minus: _____ / _____

Penalties in Minutes: _____ Time on Ice: _____

GOALTENDER:

Goals Against: _____ Shots on Goal: _____

Saves: _____ Save Percentage: _____

Total Minutes: _____ W-L-T: _____

NOTES: _____

_____

_____

_____

Team:

Date: _____ Location: _____

Opponent (or Practice): _____

Score by Period: _____ _____ _____ _____ _____
                    1   2   3   OT   F

Individual:

Position: _____ Line: _____

Goals: _____ Assists: _____ Points: _____

Power Play Goals: _____ Power Play Assists: _____

Shorthanded Goals: _____ Shorthanded Assists: _____

Faceoffs: _____ Faceoff Wins: _____

Takeaways: _____ Giveaways: _____

Shots on Goal: _____ Plus/Minus: _____ / _____

Penalties in Minutes: _____ Time on Ice: _____

Goaltender:

Goals Against: _____ Shots on Goal: _____

Saves: _____ Save Percentage: _____

Total Minutes: _____ W-L-T: _____

Notes: _____

_____

_____

_____

TEAM:

Date: _____ Location: _____

Opponent (or Practice): _____

Score by Period: _____ _____ _____ _____ _____
                    1   2   3   OT   F

INDIVIDUAL:

Position: _____ Line: _____

Goals: _____ Assists: _____ Points: _____

Power Play Goals: _____ Power Play Assists: _____

Shorthanded Goals: _____ Shorthanded Assists: _____

Faceoffs: _____ Faceoff Wins: _____

Takeaways: _____ Giveaways: _____

Shots on Goal: _____ Plus/Minus: _____ / _____

Penalties in Minutes: _____ Time on Ice: _____

GOALTENDER:

Goals Against: _____ Shots on Goal: _____

Saves: _____ Save Percentage: _____

Total Minutes: _____ W-L-T: _____

NOTES: _____

_____

_____

_____

Team:

Date: _____ Location: _____

Opponent (or Practice): _____

Score by Period: _____ _____ _____ _____ _____
  1   2   3   OT   F

Individual:

Position: _____ Line: _____

Goals: _____ Assists: _____ Points: _____

Power Play Goals: _____ Power Play Assists: _____

Shorthanded Goals: _____ Shorthanded Assists: _____

Faceoffs: _____ Faceoff Wins: _____

Takeaways: _____ Giveaways: _____

Shots on Goal: _____ Plus/Minus: _____ / _____

Penalties in Minutes: _____ Time on Ice: _____

Goaltender:

Goals Against: _____ Shots on Goal: _____

Saves: _____ Save Percentage: _____

Total Minutes: _____ W-L-T: _____

Notes: _____

_____

_____

_____

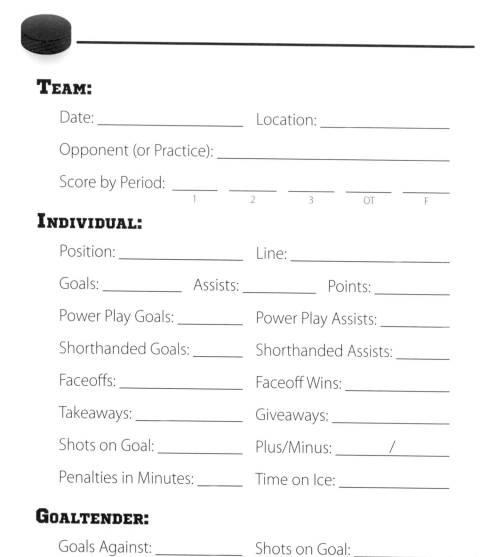

TEAM:

Date: _____ Location: _____

Opponent (or Practice): _____

Score by Period: _____ _____ _____ _____ _____
                    1   2   3   OT   F

INDIVIDUAL:

Position: _____ Line: _____

Goals: _____ Assists: _____ Points: _____

Power Play Goals: _____ Power Play Assists: _____

Shorthanded Goals: _____ Shorthanded Assists: _____

Faceoffs: _____ Faceoff Wins: _____

Takeaways: _____ Giveaways: _____

Shots on Goal: _____ Plus/Minus: _____ / _____

Penalties in Minutes: _____ Time on Ice: _____

GOALTENDER:

Goals Against: _____ Shots on Goal: _____

Saves: _____ Save Percentage: _____

Total Minutes: _____ W-L-T: _____

NOTES: _____

_____

_____

_____

NOTES/STORIES:

TEAM:

Date: _____ Location: _____

Opponent (or Practice): _____

Score by Period: _____ _____ _____ _____ _____
　　　　　　　　　　　1　　　　2　　　　3　　　OT　　　F

INDIVIDUAL:

Position: _____ Line: _____

Goals: _____ Assists: _____ Points: _____

Power Play Goals: _____ Power Play Assists: _____

Shorthanded Goals: _____ Shorthanded Assists: _____

Faceoffs: _____ Faceoff Wins: _____

Takeaways: _____ Giveaways: _____

Shots on Goal: _____ Plus/Minus: _____ / _____

Penalties in Minutes: _____ Time on Ice: _____

GOALTENDER:

Goals Against: _____ Shots on Goal: _____

Saves: _____ Save Percentage: _____

Total Minutes: _____ W-L-T: _____

NOTES: _____

_____

_____

_____

Team:

Date: _____ Location: _____

Opponent (or Practice): _____

Score by Period: _____ _____ _____ _____ _____
                    1   2   3   OT   F

Individual:

Position: _____ Line: _____

Goals: _____ Assists: _____ Points: _____

Power Play Goals: _____ Power Play Assists: _____

Shorthanded Goals: _____ Shorthanded Assists: _____

Faceoffs: _____ Faceoff Wins: _____

Takeaways: _____ Giveaways: _____

Shots on Goal: _____ Plus/Minus: _____/_____

Penalties in Minutes: _____ Time on Ice: _____

Goaltender:

Goals Against: _____ Shots on Goal: _____

Saves: _____ Save Percentage: _____

Total Minutes: _____ W-L-T: _____

Notes: _____

_____

_____

_____

TEAM:

Date: _____ Location: _____

Opponent (or Practice): _____

Score by Period: _____ _____ _____ _____ _____
　　　　　　　　　　　1　　　2　　　3　　　OT　　　F

INDIVIDUAL:

Position: _____ Line: _____

Goals: _____ Assists: _____ Points: _____

Power Play Goals: _____ Power Play Assists: _____

Shorthanded Goals: _____ Shorthanded Assists: _____

Faceoffs: _____ Faceoff Wins: _____

Takeaways: _____ Giveaways: _____

Shots on Goal: _____ Plus/Minus: _____ / _____

Penalties in Minutes: _____ Time on Ice: _____

GOALTENDER:

Goals Against: _____ Shots on Goal: _____

Saves: _____ Save Percentage: _____

Total Minutes: _____ W-L-T: _____

NOTES: _____

_____

_____

_____

TEAM:

Date: _____ Location: _____

Opponent (or Practice): _____

Score by Period: _____ _____ _____ _____ _____
                     1   2   3   OT   F

INDIVIDUAL:

Position: _____ Line: _____

Goals: _____ Assists: _____ Points: _____

Power Play Goals: _____ Power Play Assists: _____

Shorthanded Goals: _____ Shorthanded Assists: _____

Faceoffs: _____ Faceoff Wins: _____

Takeaways: _____ Giveaways: _____

Shots on Goal: _____ Plus/Minus: _____/_____

Penalties in Minutes: _____ Time on Ice: _____

GOALTENDER:

Goals Against: _____ Shots on Goal: _____

Saves: _____ Save Percentage: _____

Total Minutes: _____ W-L-T: _____

NOTES: _____

_____

_____

_____

TEAM:

Date: _____ Location: _____

Opponent (or Practice): _____

Score by Period: _____ _____ _____ _____ _____
                    1   2   3   OT   F

INDIVIDUAL:

Position: _____ Line: _____

Goals: _____ Assists: _____ Points: _____

Power Play Goals: _____ Power Play Assists: _____

Shorthanded Goals: _____ Shorthanded Assists: _____

Faceoffs: _____ Faceoff Wins: _____

Takeaways: _____ Giveaways: _____

Shots on Goal: _____ Plus/Minus: _____ / _____

Penalties in Minutes: _____ Time on Ice: _____

GOALTENDER:

Goals Against: _____ Shots on Goal: _____

Saves: _____ Save Percentage: _____

Total Minutes: _____ W-L-T: _____

NOTES: _____

_____

_____

_____

TEAM:

Date: _____ Location: _____

Opponent (or Practice): _____

Score by Period: _____ _____ _____ _____ _____
                    1   2   3   OT   F

INDIVIDUAL:

Position: _____ Line: _____

Goals: _____ Assists: _____ Points: _____

Power Play Goals: _____ Power Play Assists: _____

Shorthanded Goals: _____ Shorthanded Assists: _____

Faceoffs: _____ Faceoff Wins: _____

Takeaways: _____ Giveaways: _____

Shots on Goal: _____ Plus/Minus: _____/_____

Penalties in Minutes: _____ Time on Ice: _____

GOALTENDER:

Goals Against: _____ Shots on Goal: _____

Saves: _____ Save Percentage: _____

Total Minutes: _____ W-L-T: _____

NOTES: _____

_____

_____

_____

TEAM:

Date: _____ Location: _____

Opponent (or Practice): _____

Score by Period: _____ _____ _____ _____ _____
                    1   2   3   OT   F

INDIVIDUAL:

Position: _____ Line: _____

Goals: _____ Assists: _____ Points: _____

Power Play Goals: _____ Power Play Assists: _____

Shorthanded Goals: _____ Shorthanded Assists: _____

Faceoffs: _____ Faceoff Wins: _____

Takeaways: _____ Giveaways: _____

Shots on Goal: _____ Plus/Minus: _____ / _____

Penalties in Minutes: _____ Time on Ice: _____

GOALTENDER:

Goals Against: _____ Shots on Goal: _____

Saves: _____ Save Percentage: _____

Total Minutes: _____ W-L-T: _____

NOTES: _____

_____

_____

_____

TEAM:

Date: _____ Location: _____

Opponent (or Practice): _____

Score by Period: _____ _____ _____ _____ _____
  1   2   3   OT   F

INDIVIDUAL:

Position: _____ Line: _____

Goals: _____ Assists: _____ Points: _____

Power Play Goals: _____ Power Play Assists: _____

Shorthanded Goals: _____ Shorthanded Assists: _____

Faceoffs: _____ Faceoff Wins: _____

Takeaways: _____ Giveaways: _____

Shots on Goal: _____ Plus/Minus: _____/_____

Penalties in Minutes: _____ Time on Ice: _____

GOALTENDER:

Goals Against: _____ Shots on Goal: _____

Saves: _____ Save Percentage: _____

Total Minutes: _____ W-L-T: _____

NOTES: _____

_____

_____

_____

TEAM:

Date: _____ Location: _____

Opponent (or Practice): _____

Score by Period: _____ _____ _____ _____ _____
                    1   2   3   OT   F

INDIVIDUAL:

Position: _____ Line: _____

Goals: _____ Assists: _____ Points: _____

Power Play Goals: _____ Power Play Assists: _____

Shorthanded Goals: _____ Shorthanded Assists: _____

Faceoffs: _____ Faceoff Wins: _____

Takeaways: _____ Giveaways: _____

Shots on Goal: _____ Plus/Minus: _____ / _____

Penalties in Minutes: _____ Time on Ice: _____

GOALTENDER:

Goals Against: _____ Shots on Goal: _____

Saves: _____ Save Percentage: _____

Total Minutes: _____ W-L-T: _____

NOTES: _____

_____

_____

_____

TEAM:

Date: _____ Location: _____

Opponent (or Practice): _____

Score by Period: _____ _____ _____ _____ _____
                    1   2   3   OT   F

INDIVIDUAL:

Position: _____ Line: _____

Goals: _____ Assists: _____ Points: _____

Power Play Goals: _____ Power Play Assists: _____

Shorthanded Goals: _____ Shorthanded Assists: _____

Faceoffs: _____ Faceoff Wins: _____

Takeaways: _____ Giveaways: _____

Shots on Goal: _____ Plus/Minus: _____ / _____

Penalties in Minutes: _____ Time on Ice: _____

GOALTENDER:

Goals Against: _____ Shots on Goal: _____

Saves: _____ Save Percentage: _____

Total Minutes: _____ W-L-T: _____

NOTES: _____

_____

_____

_____

Team:

Date: _____ Location: _____

Opponent (or Practice): _____

Score by Period: _____ _____ _____ _____ _____
　　　　　　　　　　 1　　　2　　　3　　 OT　　　F

Individual:

Position: _____ Line: _____

Goals: _____ Assists: _____ Points: _____

Power Play Goals: _____ Power Play Assists: _____

Shorthanded Goals: _____ Shorthanded Assists: _____

Faceoffs: _____ Faceoff Wins: _____

Takeaways: _____ Giveaways: _____

Shots on Goal: _____ Plus/Minus: _____ / _____

Penalties in Minutes: _____ Time on Ice: _____

Goaltender:

Goals Against: _____ Shots on Goal: _____

Saves: _____ Save Percentage: _____

Total Minutes: _____ W-L-T: _____

Notes: _____

_____

_____

_____

NOTES/STORIES:

Team:

Date: _____ Location: _____

Opponent (or Practice): _____

Score by Period: _____ _____ _____ _____ _____
                        1   2   3   OT   F

Individual:

Position: _____ Line: _____

Goals: _____ Assists: _____ Points: _____

Power Play Goals: _____ Power Play Assists: _____

Shorthanded Goals: _____ Shorthanded Assists: _____

Faceoffs: _____ Faceoff Wins: _____

Takeaways: _____ Giveaways: _____

Shots on Goal: _____ Plus/Minus: _____ / _____

Penalties in Minutes: _____ Time on Ice: _____

Goaltender:

Goals Against: _____ Shots on Goal: _____

Saves: _____ Save Percentage: _____

Total Minutes: _____ W-L-T: _____

Notes: _____

_____

_____

_____

TEAM:

Date: _____ Location: _____

Opponent (or Practice): _____

Score by Period: _____ _____ _____ _____ _____
                             1   2   3   OT   F

INDIVIDUAL:

Position: _____ Line: _____

Goals: _____ Assists: _____ Points: _____

Power Play Goals: _____ Power Play Assists: _____

Shorthanded Goals: _____ Shorthanded Assists: _____

Faceoffs: _____ Faceoff Wins: _____

Takeaways: _____ Giveaways: _____

Shots on Goal: _____ Plus/Minus: _____ / _____

Penalties in Minutes: _____ Time on Ice: _____

GOALTENDER:

Goals Against: _____ Shots on Goal: _____

Saves: _____ Save Percentage: _____

Total Minutes: _____ W-L-T: _____

NOTES: _____

_____

_____

_____

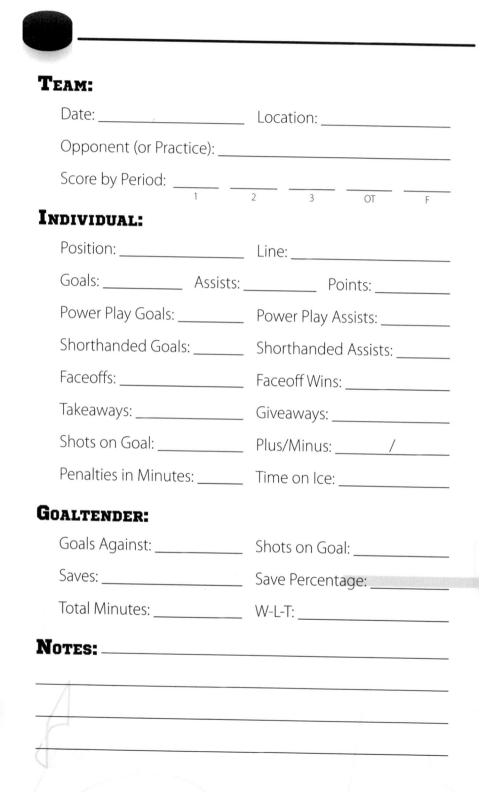

TEAM:

Date: _____ Location: _____

Opponent (or Practice): _____

Score by Period: _____ _____ _____ _____ _____
    1   2   3   OT   F

INDIVIDUAL:

Position: _____ Line: _____

Goals: _____ Assists: _____ Points: _____

Power Play Goals: _____ Power Play Assists: _____

Shorthanded Goals: _____ Shorthanded Assists: _____

Faceoffs: _____ Faceoff Wins: _____

Takeaways: _____ Giveaways: _____

Shots on Goal: _____ Plus/Minus: _____ / _____

Penalties in Minutes: _____ Time on Ice: _____

GOALTENDER:

Goals Against: _____ Shots on Goal: _____

Saves: _____ Save Percentage: _____

Total Minutes: _____ W-L-T: _____

NOTES: _____

_____

_____

_____

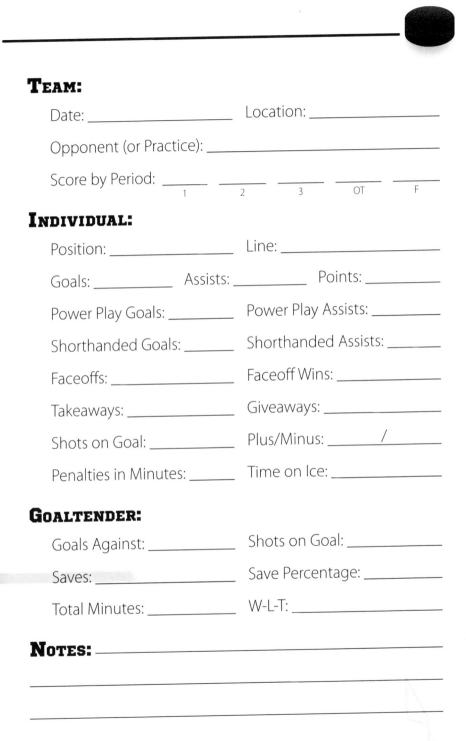

TEAM:

Date: _____ Location: _____

Opponent (or Practice): _____

Score by Period: _____ _____ _____ _____ _____
                    1   2   3   OT   F

INDIVIDUAL:

Position: _____ Line: _____

Goals: _____ Assists: _____ Points: _____

Power Play Goals: _____ Power Play Assists: _____

Shorthanded Goals: _____ Shorthanded Assists: _____

Faceoffs: _____ Faceoff Wins: _____

Takeaways: _____ Giveaways: _____

Shots on Goal: _____ Plus/Minus: _____/_____

Penalties in Minutes: _____ Time on Ice: _____

GOALTENDER:

Goals Against: _____ Shots on Goal: _____

Saves: _____ Save Percentage: _____

Total Minutes: _____ W-L-T: _____

NOTES: _____

_____

_____

_____

TEAM:

Date: _____ Location: _____

Opponent (or Practice): _____

Score by Period: _____ _____ _____ _____ _____
                        1   2   3   OT   F

INDIVIDUAL:

Position: _____ Line: _____

Goals: _____ Assists: _____ Points: _____

Power Play Goals: _____ Power Play Assists: _____

Shorthanded Goals: _____ Shorthanded Assists: _____

Faceoffs: _____ Faceoff Wins: _____

Takeaways: _____ Giveaways: _____

Shots on Goal: _____ Plus/Minus: _____ / _____

Penalties in Minutes: _____ Time on Ice: _____

GOALTENDER:

Goals Against: _____ Shots on Goal: _____

Saves: _____ Save Percentage: _____

Total Minutes: _____ W-L-T: _____

NOTES: _____

_____

_____

_____

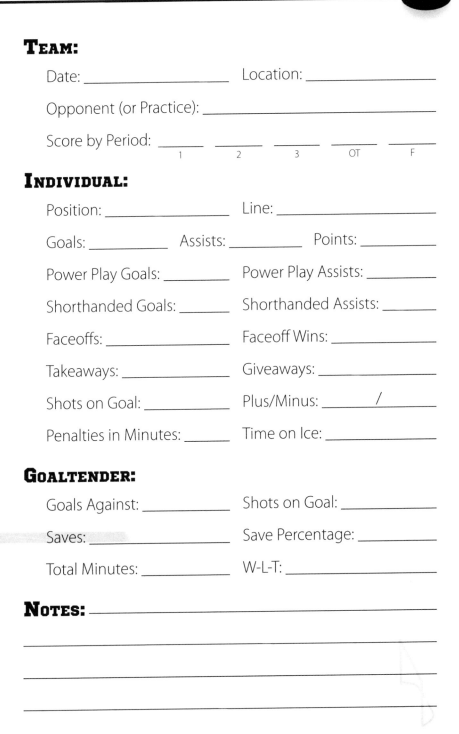

TEAM:

Date: _____ Location: _____

Opponent (or Practice): _____

Score by Period: _____ _____ _____ _____ _____
                               1   2   3   OT   F

INDIVIDUAL:

Position: _____ Line: _____

Goals: _____ Assists: _____ Points: _____

Power Play Goals: _____ Power Play Assists: _____

Shorthanded Goals: _____ Shorthanded Assists: _____

Faceoffs: _____ Faceoff Wins: _____

Takeaways: _____ Giveaways: _____

Shots on Goal: _____ Plus/Minus: _____ / _____

Penalties in Minutes: _____ Time on Ice: _____

GOALTENDER:

Goals Against: _____ Shots on Goal: _____

Saves: _____ Save Percentage: _____

Total Minutes: _____ W-L-T: _____

NOTES: _____

_____

_____

_____

TEAM:

Date: _____ Location: _____

Opponent (or Practice): _____

Score by Period: _____ _____ _____ _____ _____
                      1   2   3   OT   F

INDIVIDUAL:

Position: _____ Line: _____

Goals: _____ Assists: _____ Points: _____

Power Play Goals: _____ Power Play Assists: _____

Shorthanded Goals: _____ Shorthanded Assists: _____

Faceoffs: _____ Faceoff Wins: _____

Takeaways: _____ Giveaways: _____

Shots on Goal: _____ Plus/Minus: _____ / _____

Penalties in Minutes: _____ Time on Ice: _____

GOALTENDER:

Goals Against: _____ Shots on Goal: _____

Saves: _____ Save Percentage: _____

Total Minutes: _____ W-L-T: _____

NOTES: _____

_____

_____

_____

Team:

Date: _____ Location: _____

Opponent (or Practice): _____

Score by Period: _____ _____ _____ _____ _____
                      1   2   3   OT   F

Individual:

Position: _____ Line: _____

Goals: _____ Assists: _____ Points: _____

Power Play Goals: _____ Power Play Assists: _____

Shorthanded Goals: _____ Shorthanded Assists: _____

Faceoffs: _____ Faceoff Wins: _____

Takeaways: _____ Giveaways: _____

Shots on Goal: _____ Plus/Minus: _____/_____

Penalties in Minutes: _____ Time on Ice: _____

Goaltender:

Goals Against: _____ Shots on Goal: _____

Saves: _____ Save Percentage: _____

Total Minutes: _____ W-L-T: _____

Notes: _____

_____

_____

_____

TEAM:

Date: _____ Location: _____

Opponent (or Practice): _____

Score by Period: _____ _____ _____ _____ _____
                      1   2   3   OT   F

INDIVIDUAL:

Position: _____ Line: _____

Goals: _____ Assists: _____ Points: _____

Power Play Goals: _____ Power Play Assists: _____

Shorthanded Goals: _____ Shorthanded Assists: _____

Faceoffs: _____ Faceoff Wins: _____

Takeaways: _____ Giveaways: _____

Shots on Goal: _____ Plus/Minus: _____ / _____

Penalties in Minutes: _____ Time on Ice: _____

GOALTENDER:

Goals Against: _____ Shots on Goal: _____

Saves: _____ Save Percentage: _____

Total Minutes: _____ W-L-T: _____

NOTES: _____

_____

_____

_____

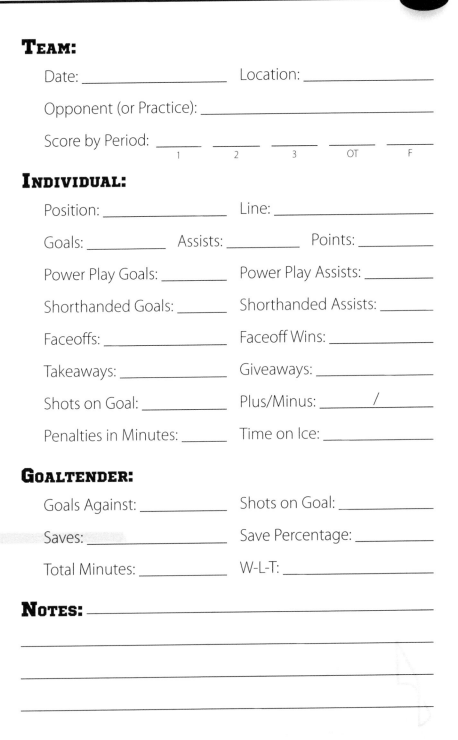

TEAM:

Date: _____ Location: _____

Opponent (or Practice): _____

Score by Period: _____ _____ _____ _____ _____
                    1   2   3   OT   F

INDIVIDUAL:

Position: _____ Line: _____

Goals: _____ Assists: _____ Points: _____

Power Play Goals: _____ Power Play Assists: _____

Shorthanded Goals: _____ Shorthanded Assists: _____

Faceoffs: _____ Faceoff Wins: _____

Takeaways: _____ Giveaways: _____

Shots on Goal: _____ Plus/Minus: _____/_____

Penalties in Minutes: _____ Time on Ice: _____

GOALTENDER:

Goals Against: _____ Shots on Goal: _____

Saves: _____ Save Percentage: _____

Total Minutes: _____ W-L-T: _____

NOTES: _____

_____

_____

_____

TEAM:

Date: _____ Location: _____

Opponent (or Practice): _____

Score by Period: _____ _____ _____ _____ _____
                   1   2   3   OT   F

INDIVIDUAL:

Position: _____ Line: _____

Goals: _____ Assists: _____ Points: _____

Power Play Goals: _____ Power Play Assists: _____

Shorthanded Goals: _____ Shorthanded Assists: _____

Faceoffs: _____ Faceoff Wins: _____

Takeaways: _____ Giveaways: _____

Shots on Goal: _____ Plus/Minus: _____ / _____

Penalties in Minutes: _____ Time on Ice: _____

GOALTENDER:

Goals Against: _____ Shots on Goal: _____

Saves: _____ Save Percentage: _____

Total Minutes: _____ W-L-T: _____

NOTES: _____

_____

_____

_____

NOTES/STORIES:

TEAM:

Date: _____ Location: _____

Opponent (or Practice): _____

Score by Period: _____ _____ _____ _____ _____

         1   2   3   OT   F

INDIVIDUAL:

Position: _____ Line: _____

Goals: _____ Assists: _____ Points: _____

Power Play Goals: _____ Power Play Assists: _____

Shorthanded Goals: _____ Shorthanded Assists: _____

Faceoffs: _____ Faceoff Wins: _____

Takeaways: _____ Giveaways: _____

Shots on Goal: _____ Plus/Minus: _____ / _____

Penalties in Minutes: _____ Time on Ice: _____

GOALTENDER:

Goals Against: _____ Shots on Goal: _____

Saves: _____ Save Percentage: _____

Total Minutes: _____ W-L-T: _____

NOTES: _____

_____

_____

_____

TEAM:

Date: _____ Location: _____

Opponent (or Practice): _____

Score by Period: _____ _____ _____ _____ _____
⠀⠀⠀⠀⠀⠀⠀⠀⠀⠀⠀⠀⠀⠀1⠀⠀⠀⠀2⠀⠀⠀⠀3⠀⠀⠀OT⠀⠀⠀⠀F

INDIVIDUAL:

Position: _____ Line: _____

Goals: _____ Assists: _____ Points: _____

Power Play Goals: _____ Power Play Assists: _____

Shorthanded Goals: _____ Shorthanded Assists: _____

Faceoffs: _____ Faceoff Wins: _____

Takeaways: _____ Giveaways: _____

Shots on Goal: _____ Plus/Minus: _____ / _____

Penalties in Minutes: _____ Time on Ice: _____

GOALTENDER:

Goals Against: _____ Shots on Goal: _____

Saves: _____ Save Percentage: _____

Total Minutes: _____ W-L-T: _____

NOTES: _____

_____

_____

_____

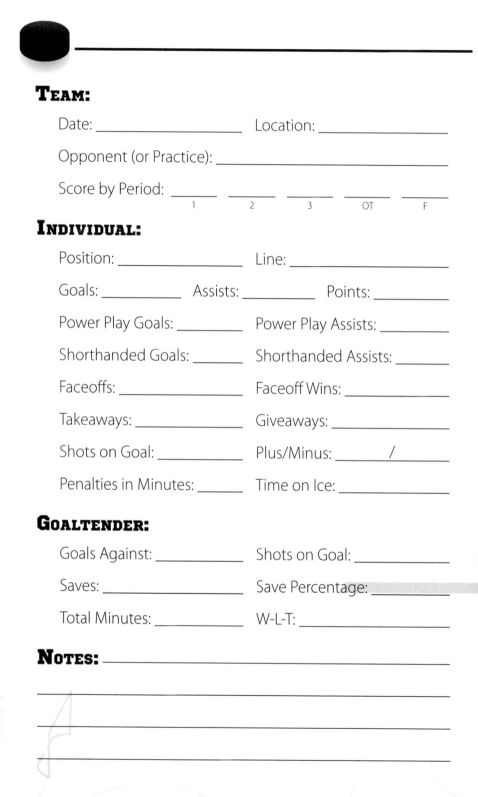

TEAM:

Date: _____ Location: _____

Opponent (or Practice): _____

Score by Period: _____ _____ _____ _____ _____
        1   2   3   OT   F

INDIVIDUAL:

Position: _____ Line: _____

Goals: _____ Assists: _____ Points: _____

Power Play Goals: _____ Power Play Assists: _____

Shorthanded Goals: _____ Shorthanded Assists: _____

Faceoffs: _____ Faceoff Wins: _____

Takeaways: _____ Giveaways: _____

Shots on Goal: _____ Plus/Minus: _____ / _____

Penalties in Minutes: _____ Time on Ice: _____

GOALTENDER:

Goals Against: _____ Shots on Goal: _____

Saves: _____ Save Percentage: _____

Total Minutes: _____ W-L-T: _____

NOTES: _____

_____

_____

_____

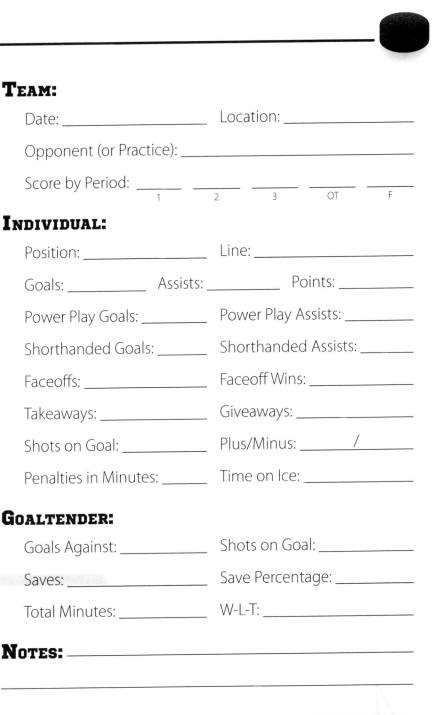

TEAM:

Date: _____ Location: _____

Opponent (or Practice): _____

Score by Period: _____ _____ _____ _____ _____
　　　　　　　　　　　　1　　　2　　　3　　　OT　　　F

INDIVIDUAL:

Position: _____ Line: _____

Goals: _____ Assists: _____ Points: _____

Power Play Goals: _____ Power Play Assists: _____

Shorthanded Goals: _____ Shorthanded Assists: _____

Faceoffs: _____ Faceoff Wins: _____

Takeaways: _____ Giveaways: _____

Shots on Goal: _____ Plus/Minus: _____/_____

Penalties in Minutes: _____ Time on Ice: _____

GOALTENDER:

Goals Against: _____ Shots on Goal: _____

Saves: _____ Save Percentage: _____

Total Minutes: _____ W-L-T: _____

NOTES: _____

_____

_____

_____

TEAM:

Date: _____ Location: _____

Opponent (or Practice): _____

Score by Period: _____ _____ _____ _____ _____
                    1   2   3   OT   F

INDIVIDUAL:

Position: _____ Line: _____

Goals: _____ Assists: _____ Points: _____

Power Play Goals: _____ Power Play Assists: _____

Shorthanded Goals: _____ Shorthanded Assists: _____

Faceoffs: _____ Faceoff Wins: _____

Takeaways: _____ Giveaways: _____

Shots on Goal: _____ Plus/Minus: _____/_____

Penalties in Minutes: _____ Time on Ice: _____

GOALTENDER:

Goals Against: _____ Shots on Goal: _____

Saves: _____ Save Percentage: _____

Total Minutes: _____ W-L-T: _____

NOTES: _____

_____

_____

_____

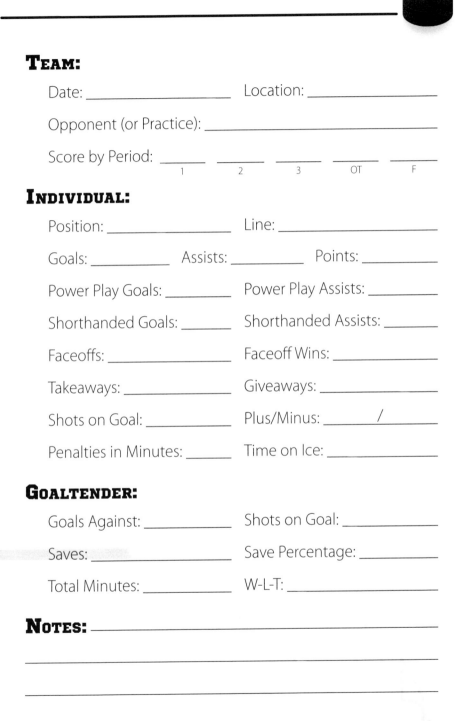

TEAM:

Date: _____ Location: _____

Opponent (or Practice): _____

Score by Period: _____ _____ _____ _____ _____
1   2   3   OT   F

INDIVIDUAL:

Position: _____ Line: _____

Goals: _____ Assists: _____ Points: _____

Power Play Goals: _____ Power Play Assists: _____

Shorthanded Goals: _____ Shorthanded Assists: _____

Faceoffs: _____ Faceoff Wins: _____

Takeaways: _____ Giveaways: _____

Shots on Goal: _____ Plus/Minus: _____ / _____

Penalties in Minutes: _____ Time on Ice: _____

GOALTENDER:

Goals Against: _____ Shots on Goal: _____

Saves: _____ Save Percentage: _____

Total Minutes: _____ W-L-T: _____

NOTES: _____

_____

_____

_____

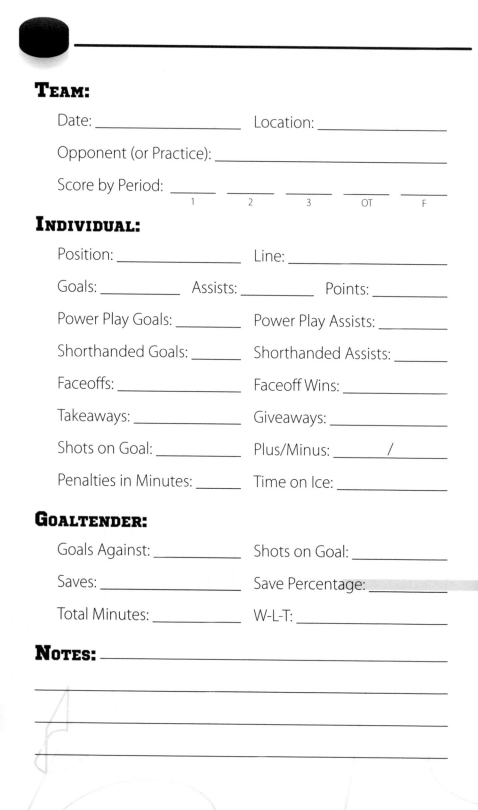

TEAM:

Date: _____ Location: _____

Opponent (or Practice): _____

Score by Period: _____ _____ _____ _____ _____
                     1   2   3   OT   F

INDIVIDUAL:

Position: _____ Line: _____

Goals: _____ Assists: _____ Points: _____

Power Play Goals: _____ Power Play Assists: _____

Shorthanded Goals: _____ Shorthanded Assists: _____

Faceoffs: _____ Faceoff Wins: _____

Takeaways: _____ Giveaways: _____

Shots on Goal: _____ Plus/Minus: _____ / _____

Penalties in Minutes: _____ Time on Ice: _____

GOALTENDER:

Goals Against: _____ Shots on Goal: _____

Saves: _____ Save Percentage: _____

Total Minutes: _____ W-L-T: _____

NOTES: _____

_____

_____

_____

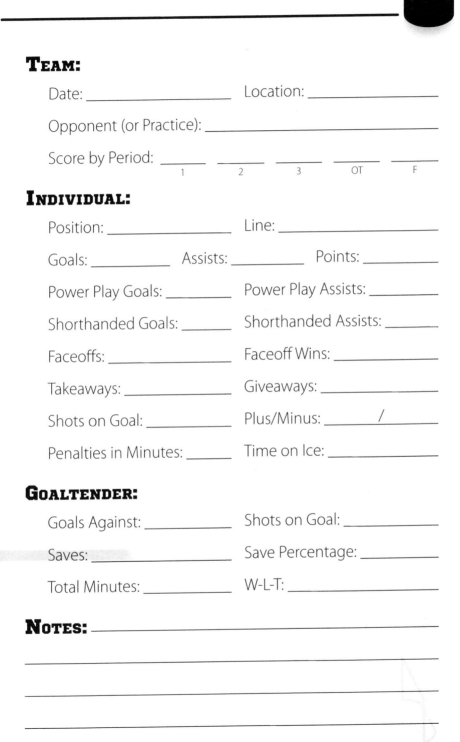

TEAM:

Date: _____ Location: _____

Opponent (or Practice): _____

Score by Period: _____ _____ _____ _____ _____
1   2   3   OT   F

INDIVIDUAL:

Position: _____ Line: _____

Goals: _____ Assists: _____ Points: _____

Power Play Goals: _____ Power Play Assists: _____

Shorthanded Goals: _____ Shorthanded Assists: _____

Faceoffs: _____ Faceoff Wins: _____

Takeaways: _____ Giveaways: _____

Shots on Goal: _____ Plus/Minus: _____/_____

Penalties in Minutes: _____ Time on Ice: _____

GOALTENDER:

Goals Against: _____ Shots on Goal: _____

Saves: _____ Save Percentage: _____

Total Minutes: _____ W-L-T: _____

NOTES: _____

_____

_____

_____

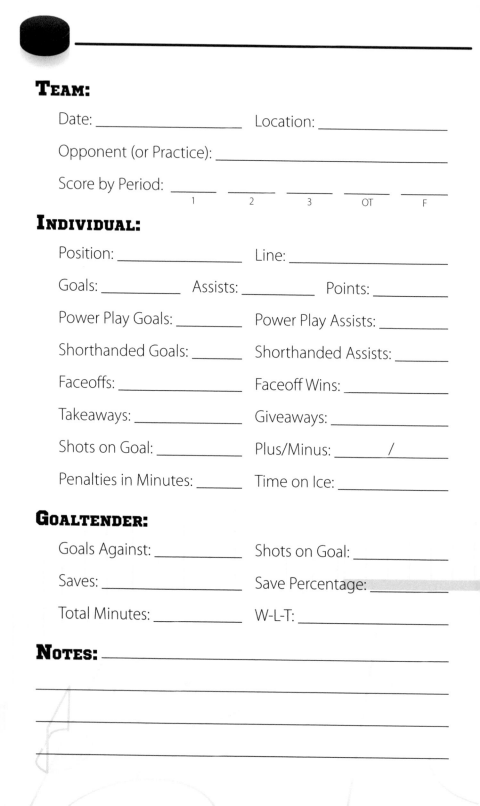

TEAM:

Date: _____ Location: _____

Opponent (or Practice): _____

Score by Period: _____ _____ _____ _____ _____
$\quad\quad\quad\quad\quad\quad\quad$ 1 $\quad\quad$ 2 $\quad\quad$ 3 $\quad\quad$ OT $\quad\quad$ F

INDIVIDUAL:

Position: _____ Line: _____

Goals: _____ Assists: _____ Points: _____

Power Play Goals: _____ Power Play Assists: _____

Shorthanded Goals: _____ Shorthanded Assists: _____

Faceoffs: _____ Faceoff Wins: _____

Takeaways: _____ Giveaways: _____

Shots on Goal: _____ Plus/Minus: _____ / _____

Penalties in Minutes: _____ Time on Ice: _____

GOALTENDER:

Goals Against: _____ Shots on Goal: _____

Saves: _____ Save Percentage: _____

Total Minutes: _____ W-L-T: _____

NOTES: _____

_____

_____

_____

TEAM:

Date: _____   Location: _____

Opponent (or Practice): _____

Score by Period: _____ _____ _____ _____ _____
　　　　　　　　　　　1　　　　2　　　　3　　　　OT　　　　F

INDIVIDUAL:

Position: _____   Line: _____

Goals: _____   Assists: _____   Points: _____

Power Play Goals: _____   Power Play Assists: _____

Shorthanded Goals: _____   Shorthanded Assists: _____

Faceoffs: _____   Faceoff Wins: _____

Takeaways: _____   Giveaways: _____

Shots on Goal: _____   Plus/Minus: _____ / _____

Penalties in Minutes: _____   Time on Ice: _____

GOALTENDER:

Goals Against: _____   Shots on Goal: _____

Saves: _____   Save Percentage: _____

Total Minutes: _____   W-L-T: _____

NOTES: _____

_____

_____

_____

NOTES/STORIES:

NOTES/STORIES:

Autographs ———————————————————

Autographs

Autographs ———————————————————————

Autographs

Autographs ───────────────